the Sourdough Bible

10 in 1

THE ULTIMATE GUIDE FOR BEGINNERS TO BAKE THE PERFECT LOAF. 365 DAYS OF RECIPES FOR DOUGH, CAKES, AND BAKED GOODS TO BECOME THE GO-TO BAKER OF FAMILY AND FRIENDS

ARE YOU A BUSY MOM OR A CAREER-DRIVEN WOMAN DREAMING OF HAVING EVERYTHING UNDER CONTROL?

DO YOU WANT TO LOSE WEIGHT AND PREPARE TASTY, AFFORDABLE, AND QUICK MEALS WITHOUT LOSING YOUR MIND IN THE KITCHEN?

You find yourself running from one commitment to another, **always stressed**, and between work, family, and household duties, it feels **like there's never any time for you.**

Maybe you also want to **lose some weight**, but bland food and extreme diets are **slowly killing your soul.**

<u>You look in the mirror and feel a disconnect, as if your body doesn't reflect who you truly are inside.</u>

You try to cook healthily, but every time you find yourself grabbing something ready from the freezer or ordering takeout. You dream of preparing healthy and tasty meals that your family will love, but it feels like a Herculean task.

Have you ever wondered what your life would be like if you could eat delicious foods that also help you lose weight, without spending hours in the kitchen?

If you could find a balance between work, relationships, and self-care without constantly feeling guilty?

The solution isn't an extreme diet or another fitness app - it's a comprehensive guide that addresses the specific problems you have. A guide that speaks your language and directly addresses YOU.

Here's what you can discover with this guide:

☑ Unlock the simple method **to balance your work, relationships, and personal care**, and leave behind the guilt and stress;

☑ Discover the secrets to **balancing work, relationships, and self-care without the guilt, stress, or kitchen hassle**;

☑ Learn the magic of cooking techniques that allow you to savor your favorite dishes while **staying on track with your weight loss goals**

☑ Explore why quick-fix solutions often fail and how a blend of effective methods can lead you to real and **lasting transformation**

☑ Reveal the one mindset shift that can **break the cycle of failure and frustration**, paving the way for lasting success

☑ Learn why that time-saving meal or gym alternative might be **hindering your progress** and what you can do instead

☑ **...and much, much more!!**

Even if your days are filled with responsibilities, you've never cooked before, or you think that healthy cooking is expensive, this book offers a fresh approach to finally attain your cooking and fitness goals.

Don't waste another moment on quick fixes and empty promises.

SCAN THE QR CODE BELOW AND BEGIN YOUR JOURNEY TOWARDS A HEALTHIER, HAPPIER, AND MORE BALANCED LIFE.

THE SOURDOUGH BIBLE
THE ULTIMATE GUIDE FOR BEGINNERS TO BAKE THE PERFECT LOAF. 365 DAYS OF RECIPES FOR DOUGH, CAKES, AND BAKED GOODS TO BECOME THE GO-TO BAKER OF FAMILY AND FRIENDS

First Edition June 2023

TABLE OF CONTENTS

CHAPTER 3
TROUBLESHOOTING

CHAPTER 4
NUTRITION AND HEALTH BENEFITS

CHAPTER 5
BASIC SOURDOUGH BREAD RECIPES

CHAPTER 6
ARTISAN BASIC SOURDOUGH BREADS

CHAPTER 7
RUSTIC RECIPES

CHAPTER 8
PIZZA DOUGH AND FLATBREADS

CHAPTER 9
WHOLE GRAIN RECIPES

CHAPTER 10
DESSERTS

CHAPTER 11
GLUTEN-FREE

CHAPTER 12
SOURDOUGH DISCARD RECIPES

CHAPTER 13
QUICK BREADS AND PANCAKES   131

THE SOURDOUGH BIBLE

The Ultimate Guide for Beginners to Bake the Perfect Loaf. 365 Days of Recipes for Dough, Cakes, and Baked Goods to Become the Go-to Baker of Family and Friends

---

STELLA BROWN

INTRODUCTION

Here in the realm of sourdough, time-honored customs and cutting-edge cuisine come together in delicious harmony. The Sourdough Bible is the final word on fermented dough, revealing all the techniques and tricks of this time-honored baking method. This book will guide you, baker veteran or interested newcomer, on an educational adventure into the fascinating world of sourdough bread.

For many people, making bread with sourdough starter is more than simply a passing fad. The long history of sourdough and the symbiotic link between people and the microbes responsible for transforming simple ingredients into a tasty, healthy, and readily digestible staple are emblematic of our inherent connection to the land and to each other. The joy of feeding oneself and one's loved ones on homemade, healthful bread has been lost in a society where processed and fast foods reign supreme.

The journey through the heart and mind of sourdough awaits you behind the covers of The Sourdough Bible. Everything you need to know to make and keep a sourdough starter culture, from the biology of wild yeasts and lactobacilli to how to do it, is laid out clearly and enthusiastically. Learn how to make bread with the ideal rise, crumb, and crust by delving into the specifics of flours, hydration ratios, fermentation periods, and the influence of temperature.

But this book is about more than just bread; it's an open invitation to explore the many uses of sourdough. Explore the world of sour pancakes, savory muffins, and delicate pastries that can be made with your active starting. Experience the transformational power of time in the kitchen by exploring the entrancing spectrum of flavors that emerges through lengthy, slow fermentation.

Along the way, we'll offer anecdotes, hints, and techniques from seasoned bakers so that you'll have a wealth of knowledge at your disposal. The Sourdough Bible is meant to be your constant companion, with detailed directions, troubleshooting help, and a wealth of delectable recipes that highlight the many uses for sourdough.

The Sourdough Bible is your trustworthy companion on your journey to perfect crusty loaves, successful rises, and the pleasure of sharing your creations with loved ones. Come with us on this adventure to see what happens when you mix flour, water, and time together. Join me on a sourdough quest as I discover the key to making bread that satisfies not just the stomach but the spirit as well.

You have found The Sourdough Bible, your gateway to the wonderful world of sourdough.

CHAPTER 1
THE HISTORY AND SCIENCE OF SOURDOUGH

In a world where the pace of life seems to accelerate with each passing day, finding moments of respite and connection becomes increasingly vital. The quest for balance and fulfillment takes on new meaning as we navigate through a whirlwind of responsibilities and obligations. Amidst this speedy life pace, it is essential to discover activities that provide solace, a sense of accomplishment, and a connection to something timeless.

One such activity that has captured the hearts and kitchens of people worldwide is sourdough bread baking. Beyond the hustle and bustle of our daily lives, this craft offers a tranquil retreat—a chance to slow down, engage our senses, and create something truly extraordinary.

The beauty of sourdough lies not only in the process but also in the shared experiences it fosters. From the moment you create your first bubbling sourdough starter to the aroma that fills your home as the loaves rise and bake, every step is an invitation to slow down, appreciate the present moment, and indulge in the magic of transformation.

Beyond its status as a social media sensation, sourdough bread has long captured the attention of microbiologists around the world. Researchers in Melbourne, alongside their international counterparts, have delved deep into the science behind sourdough. Despite all sourdough loaves beginning with the same basic ingredients - flour and water - their end results are remarkably diverse. This is due to the intricate interplay

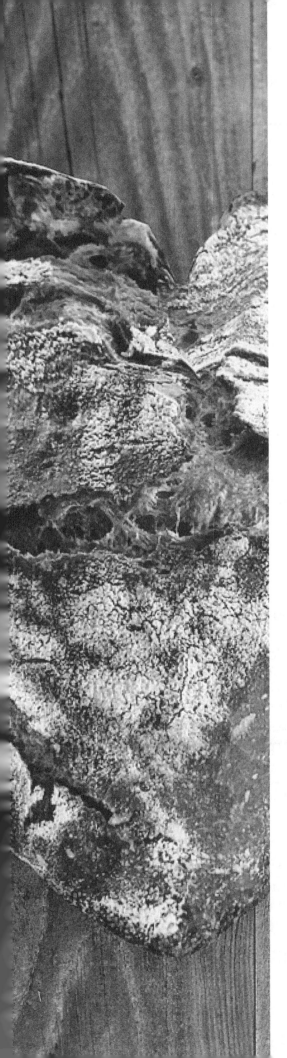

between unique yeasts and bacteria that inhabit the starters, creating a symphony of flavors and textures.

For scientists, the microbial communities in sourdough starters hold significant importance in the realm of agricultural research. Environmental factors such as temperature, humidity, and even the local flora and fauna influence the development and characteristics of these microbial communities. This gives rise to regional variations in sourdough, making each loaf a reflection of its specific time and place.

While the flavors of sourdough bread are undoubtedly shaped by the microbial composition, it goes beyond that. The recipe itself, the parameters of the culture, and even the consistency of the starter all play a role. A stiffer starter, with less water content, produces a denser crumb and a more pronounced tang. Conversely, a runnier starter results in a lighter, airier loaf with a milder flavor profile. These subtle nuances highlight the intricate dance between ingredients, microbes, and technique.

Moreover, the history of sourdough bread stretches back centuries, transcending borders and cultures. From the ancient Egyptians who stumbled upon the magic of wild yeasts to the Greeks who refined the art of bread baking, sourdough has traversed time and geography. It made its way to France in the 17th century, where bakers perfected their techniques, and later journeyed across the Atlantic to California during the Gold Rush, leaving an indelible mark on the culture of San Francisco.

The long and varied history of sourdough bread spans countless countries and civilizations. Sourdough has played a crucial role in the development of cuisines all over the world, from its ancient Egyptian origins to its predominance in many civilizations throughout history. Ancient Egypt is the first known location where sourdough was made and used. The Egyptians learned about the leavening potential of wild yeast around 1500 BCE. They discovered that if they mixed flour and water and let it ferment, the dough would rise, making for fluffier and tastier bread. After realizing that wild yeast and lactic acid bacteria could be cultured, sourdough starters were developed for use in the perpetual leavening of bread.

Sourdough baking techniques evolved alongside expanding civilizations. The ancient Greeks and Romans, for instance, embraced and perfected the craft of bread making through trial and error with a variety of flours, yeasts, and shaping techniques. As time went on, sourdough bread became an integral part of these cultures' diets.

Sourdough's global dissemination was greatly aided by the development of extensive trading networks. The Silk Road enabled the communication and interchange of ideas, innovations, and cultural practices between Europe and Asia. The knowledge of sourdough fermentation was carried across great distances by merchants and adventurers. Because of this, bread cultures across the globe have become increasingly varied, with several regional adaptations of sourdough.

Sourdough has become increasingly linked to pivotal moments in recent history. During the mid-19th century California Gold Rush, sourdough was an essential part of the diet of the miners and settlers. In such a harsh and sparse setting, it provided dependable sustenance. The sourdough starter was the miners' last hope for fresh bread, so much so that they often slept with it to keep it warm.

During wartime and food shortages, sourdough also played an important role. During World War II, when yeast was in short supply due to food rationing, sourdough was a useful alternative. Home bakers and commercial bakeries alike could not produce bread, muffins, and other baked items without their sourdough starters. During difficult times, sourdough came to represent fortitude and flexibility in the face of hardship.

There has been a significant increase in sourdough's popularity in recent years. The long fermentation process, distinctive flavors, and health advantages of sourdough have captivated artisanal bakers and home fans alike. With the advent of the internet and various social media platforms, a thriving and mutually supportive community of sourdough bakers has emerged to share recipes, methods, and personal tales.

Our respect for the intricacy of the sourdough fermentation process has grown as our scientific knowledge has expanded. Further investigation into fermentation's microbial interactions is illuminating the wide variety of yeast and bacterium strains seen in sourdough starters. This research furthers our understanding of how sourdough affects digestive health, how flavor develops in it, and what nutrients it contains.

Sourdough bread is still a treasured culinary tradition today. People from all walks of life can't get enough of its fascinating past, vital cultural value, and unique flavors. The legacy of sourdough, whether it's the tart San Francisco variety or the hearty rye sourdough of Nordic countries, remains, a reminder of the artistry and perseverance inherent in this age-old method of bread making.

In the magical realm of sourdough, microbes perform a fascinating dance that reveals the complex science underlying this age-old method of bread making. A sourdough starter contains a mini-ecosystem where yeast and lactic acid bacteria undergo a metamorphic journey.

Wild yeast gets activated from its latent state as flour and water combine to create a hospitable environment. Yeast acts like little culinary soldiers, devouring the flour's starches and converting them into sugar. Enzymes, the unseen helpers of the microbial world, assist in this sugary feast by breaking down the molecular structures of starch.

Carbon dioxide gas bubbles through the dough like a celebratory song as yeast enjoys its sugary treat. These tiny air pockets, which are held inside the gluten network, softly expand the dough and give it a fluffy mouth feel. This entrancing expansion is what gives sourdough its distinctive crumb structure, which beckons us to experience the wonder of this bread for ourselves.

However, the yeast does not exist in isolation in this magical setting. Enter the lactic acid bacteria, magical beings responsible for the acidic undertones of sourdough. They too benefit from the yeast's carbohydrates, which are metabolized by them into lactic acid. This lactic acid gives the bread its signature sour flavor and adds a wonderful tang.

The relationship between yeast and lactic acid bacteria is like a well-balanced musical duet. As they coexist in the starter, they work together and compete subtly to determine the bread's final flavor. Each sourdough culture contains a distinct combination of yeast strains and bacterial species which results in bread that is both distinctive and nuanced.

The sourdough alchemy relies heavily on temperature and time, the watchdogs of this microbiological realm. Yeast and bacteria thrive within the appropriate temperature range, often between 20 and 30 degrees Celsius (68 and 86 degrees Fahrenheit), while undesirable invaders are kept at bay. Fermentation is an exercise in patience that yields a culinary masterpiece by allowing the dough's flavors to develop and mature.

The science behind sourdough's delicious flavor also has health benefits. Complex carbs are broken down throughout the lengthy fermentation process, making them more easily absorbed by the body. It also makes more nutrients available to the body, increasing their absorption and utilization.

The magic and allure of sourdough lies in the harmony of flavor and texture orchestrated by the unseen powers of yeast and lactic acid bacteria. It's proof that the microscopic world of nature, where scientific knowledge and culinary pleasure meet, is just as beautiful as the macroscopic one. So, when you enjoy each slice of sourdough bread, think about the fascinating science and fascinating story that lay under its simple crust.

In the present day, as we navigate the uncertainties of a global pandemic, sourdough baking offers more than just delicious bread. It provides a connection to our culinary heritage, a source of comfort and creativity, and a tangible way to nurture our well-being. The act of tending to a sourdough starter, observing its rise and fall, and transforming it into a loaf of bread is a ritual that grounds us amidst the chaos of the world.

As we embark on this journey of sourdough exploration, let us embrace the artistry and science behind it. May we find joy in the process, connection with our ancestors who once kneaded dough in ancient civilizations, and a profound appreciation for the transformative power of flour, water, and time. Let the magic of sourdough unfold before us as we knead, shape, and bake our way to delicious and soul-nourishing loaves. In each slice of bread, we taste not just the flavors of fermentation but also the resilience and ingenuity of humanity.

As you begin your exploration of sourdough bread, may you discover joy in the process, connect with a heritage steeped in culinary traditions, and develop a profound appreciation for the transformative qualities of flour, water, and time. Witness the enchantment of sourdough unfold as you engage in the activities of kneading, shaping, and baking, resulting in delicious and nourishing loaves that satisfy both the palate and the soul. Prepare yourself for a journey that not only delights your taste buds but also awakens your senses and ignites your passion for the timeless craft of sourdough baking.

To conclude, sourdough bread carries a wealth of history that traverses continents and centuries. From its accidental discovery in ancient Egypt to its present-day popularity, sourdough remains a beloved and diverse culinary tradition cherished by bakers and bread enthusiasts alike.

CHAPTER 2
THE SOURDOUGH BAKING PROCESS

Starting to learn how to make sourdough bread may feel daunting, similar to picking up a new language. It goes beyond following simple instructions, as sourdough bread recipes involve formulas and schedules. Understanding each step, including how to interpret and create these formulas, is key. This knowledge not only enables you to follow recipes but also empowers you to develop your own preferred techniques.

By understanding the following key elements of sourdough bread-making, you can embark on a journey of exploration, honing your skills and creating delicious loaves of bread with unique flavors and textures:

2.1 FERMENTATION CULTURE

In the heart of the baker's kitchen, a living entity breathes and pulsates with the magic of fermentation. This mystical creation is none other than the sourdough starter—a captivating world of microscopic organisms, teeming with wild yeast and friendly bacteria. It is a living ecosystem that holds the key to the enchanting alchemy of sourdough bread.

Imagine a humble mixture of flour and water, gently combined in a simple jar. As if by some ancient spell, this innocuous blend becomes a haven for microorganisms seeking nourishment and companionship. In this symbiotic relationship, the

flour provides food for the organisms, while the organisms, in turn, impart flavor, texture, and rise to the bread.

Within the depths of the sourdough starter, a symphony of microbial activity unfolds. Wild yeast, known as Saccharomyces exiguus, awakens from its slumber, hungrily devouring the sugars present in the flour. As it feasts, it produces carbon dioxide, the invisible force that gives bread its ethereal rise. It is the wild yeast that imparts the distinct tang and complexity to sourdough bread, transforming a mere loaf into a culinary masterpiece.

But the yeast is not alone in this miraculous transformation. Lactobacilli bacteria, such as Lactobacillus sanfranciscensis, join the microbial orchestra. These friendly bacteria, with their lactic acid-producing prowess, bring a delightful tang to the bread's flavor profile. They work in harmony with the yeast, creating an environment that favors the development of a unique and sought-after sourdough taste.

As the days pass, the sourdough starter develops its character, a testament to the baker's care and dedication. The balance between yeast and bacteria is nurtured through regular feedings, where a portion of the starter is discarded and replaced with fresh flour and water. This ritual ensures that the microorganisms remain vibrant and active, ready to breathe life into each batch of bread.

The sourdough starter becomes more than a mere ingredient; it becomes a trusted companion, a living being that connects the baker to the ancient traditions of bread-making. It carries the history and lineage of countless loaves, passed down through generations. Each baker's starter is unique, reflecting the environment, flour, and personal touch that shapes its character.

In the gentle embrace of the baker's hands, the starter comes alive, its silky texture and slightly tangy aroma captivating the senses. It becomes the foundation upon which the art of sourdough bread is built. With each feeding, the starter grows in strength and vitality, its bubbles of fermentation a testament to the vibrant life it harbors.

And so, the sourdough starter becomes more than a simple mixture of flour and water. It is a living entity that holds the secrets of fermentation, the gateway to artisanal bread-making. It represents the beauty of simplicity, where humble ingredients transform into something extraordinary through time, patience, and the alchemical power of nature.

As the baker embarks on their sourdough journey, they learn to listen to the whispers of the starter, to interpret its moods and needs. They become attuned to its cycles, observing the rise and fall, the aroma, and the bubbles that dance upon its surface. They cultivate a bond, a kinship with the starter, as they embark on a shared adventure of creation.

In the world of sourdough, the starter holds the key to unlocking the mysteries of flavor, texture, and artisanal craftsmanship. It is a living testament to the marvels of nature, a reminder of the interconnectedness of all living things. As the baker tends to their starter with love and respect, they enter into a profound relationship, one that transcends the mere act of bread-making.

In the end, the sourdough starter becomes more than just a leavening agent; it becomes a living embodiment of the baker's passion and artistry. It is a testament to the age-old tradition of bread-making, where simple ingredients and the power of fermentation combine to create a culinary experience that nourishes both body and soul. The sourdough starter is the gateway to a world of endless possibilities, where the baker's creativity knows no bounds.

2.2 PRE-FERMENT

Within the realm of sourdough bread-making, the Pre-Ferment stands as a transformative force, a catalyst that elevates the dough to new heights. As an essential component of the sourdough process, the Pre-Ferment captures the essence of the wild yeast and friendly bacteria, infusing the bread with their captivating flavors and unparalleled rise.

Picture a small portion of the sourdough starter, carefully measured and placed into a vessel. This humble portion carries with it the living essence of the starter, a concentrated source of the microorganisms that have flourished within its depths. It is this magical mixture that is known as the Pre-Ferment—a powerhouse of fermentation and a key player in the alchemical dance of sourdough bread.

Like a master alchemist, the baker carefully nurtures the Pre-Ferment, building it up to its full potential. A precise balance of flour, water, and the starter is combined, creating an environment where the wild yeast and bacteria can thrive. As the Pre-Ferment ferments, its population of microorganisms multiplies, creating a vibrant and dynamic community within the mixture.

During this period of fermentation, the Pre-Ferment undergoes a magnificent transformation. The wild yeast, fueled by the carbohydrates in the flour, reproduces and releases carbon dioxide, filling the Pre-Ferment with tiny bubbles of gas. These bubbles contribute to the rise of the bread, creating a light and airy crumb. Meanwhile, the friendly bacteria, such as lactobacilli, work their magic, producing lactic acid that adds a subtle tang to the bread's flavor profile.

As the Pre-Ferment matures, it develops a distinct aroma, a heady mixture of yeast, acidity, and fermentation byproducts. It becomes a living entity in its own right, teeming with microscopic life and the potential to impart unparalleled flavor and texture to the bread dough. The baker's keen eye and experience guide them in determining the optimal moment to incorporate the Pre-Ferment into the bread-making process.

With each fold and gentle incorporation, the Pre-Ferment becomes an integral part of the dough, infusing it with its dynamic energy. The Pre-Ferment's microorganisms continue their work within the dough, fermenting the sugars present in the flour and releasing carbon dioxide gas. This gas, trapped within the gluten network of the dough, creates the coveted rise and structure that sets sourdough bread apart.

But the Pre-Ferment is not merely a catalyst for fermentation; it is a flavor enhancer, a maestro conducting a symphony of taste. The byproducts of fermentation, including organic acids and aromatic compounds, add depth, complexity, and a hint of tang to the bread's flavor. Each Pre-Ferment carries its own unique signature, a fingerprint of the specific strains of yeast and bacteria that inhabit it.

The baker, in their mastery of the Pre-Ferment, becomes a steward of this living culture. They carefully tend to its needs, feeding it with fresh flour and water, allowing it to continue its vibrant existence. With each feeding, the Pre-Ferment grows stronger, its microbial population flourishing, ready to bring life and character to future loaves of bread.

In the realm of sourdough bread-making, the Pre-Ferment holds the power to transform humble ingredients into works of culinary art. It is a testament to the incredible potential that lies within the simplest of mixtures. As bakers embrace the magic of the levain, they join a lineage of artisans and enthusiasts who have harnessed the power of fermentation, embracing the beauty and complexity that arise from the collaboration between humans and microorganisms.

With the Pre-Ferment as their guide, bakers embark on a journey of creativity, experimentation, and discovery. They unlock the door to a world of endless possibilities, where each Pre-Ferment brings its own unique character and nuances to the bread. The Pre-Ferment becomes a trusted companion, a partner in the quest for exceptional flavor, texture, and the soul-satisfying joy of freshly baked sourdough bread.

2.3 DOUGH INCORPORATION

The Dough Incorporation stage is where the alchemy begins. It is the process of bringing together the key ingredients—flour, water, levain, and salt—to create the dough. Mixing is not just a mechanical action; it is an art that requires a delicate balance of precision and intuition.

To commence this step, the baker combines the levain, a portion of the sourdough starter, with fresh flour and water. The levain, bursting with wild yeast and friendly bacteria, is the vital agent that imparts flavor, texture, and rise to the bread. As the levain is incorporated into the mixture, it breathes life into the dough, initiating a symphony of fermentation.

The baker's hands or a stand mixer gently knead the ingredients together, ensuring even distribution and hydration. The dough gradually forms, transitioning from a shaggy mass to a cohesive, supple texture. The process of mixing encourages the development of gluten—a network of proteins responsible for the dough's structure and elasticity.

As the dough is mixed, gluten strands begin to form, entwining and strengthening with each passing moment. The baker's touch becomes crucial in judging the dough's consistency. They aim for a delicate balance: not too sticky, indicating excess hydration, and not too stiff, signifying insufficient hydration. Experience and intuition guide the baker in attaining the perfect dough texture.

The mixing process varies depending on the baker's preference and the desired outcome. Some opt for an intensive mixing technique, incorporating long periods of vigorous kneading to encourage gluten development. Others favor a gentle approach, incorporating shorter mixing times and frequent rest intervals, allowing the dough to develop naturally.

Regardless of the chosen technique, the goal of mixing is to achieve proper hydration, gluten development, and initial distribution of the levain and salt throughout the dough. The result is a smooth, elastic mass that holds the promise of becoming a beautifully textured, flavorful loaf.

2.4 PRIMARY FERMENTATION

After the dough incorporation stage, the dough enters a period of rest and fermentation known as primary fermentation. This crucial step allows the dough to undergo a transformative journey, where flavors deepen, textures evolve, and the dough acquires its distinctive character.

During primary fermentation, the dough is placed in a covered container—a bowl or a food-grade plastic tub—to provide a controlled environment for fermentation. The dough is allowed to rest at a consistent temperature, usually room temperature or slightly warmer, to facilitate optimal fermentation.

As the dough rests, the wild yeast and bacteria within the levain go to work, metabolizing the sugars present in the flour. This process releases carbon dioxide gas, causing the dough to rise and develop a light, airy structure. Simultaneously, the bacteria produce lactic acid, contributing to the distinct tang and complexity associated with sourdough bread.

Throughout primary fermentation, the baker employs a technique called folding. This technique involves gently stretching and folding the dough at regular intervals. Folding helps to strengthen the gluten structure, redistribute fermentation byproducts, and promote even fermentation throughout the dough.

The frequency and timing of the folds depend on the dough's specific needs and the baker's intuition. Typically, the dough is folded every 30 minutes to an hour during the initial stages of primary fermentation. As the dough develops strength and structure, the frequency of folding may decrease.

The length of primary fermentation varies based on several factors, including the ambient temperature, dough hydration, and desired flavor profile. On average, primary fermentation can range from 3 to 6 hours, but some bakers opt for extended fermentation periods of 8 to 12 hours or even longer. The duration allows the flavors to deepen, producing a more pronounced sourness and complexity.

The baker closely observes the dough's progression during bulk fermentation, looking for signs of fermentation activity. Visual cues such as increased volume, air bubbles on the dough's surface, and a slightly domed appearance indicate active fermentation. Additionally, the dough's texture evolves, becoming more extensible and responsive to touch.

The baker's intuition comes into play when determining the ideal time to conclude primary fermentation. They consider factors such as fermentation activity, dough volume, and desired dough characteristics. Under fermented dough may lack flavor and structure, while over fermented dough can become overly acidic and lose its elasticity.

Upon completion of primary fermentation, the dough is ready for the next stage of bread-making, which typically involves dividing, preshaping, bench rest, and shaping the dough into its final form. These subsequent steps harness the work accomplished during mixing and primary fermentation, shaping the dough into beautiful loaves that will undergo proofing and baking.

In the realm of sourdough bread-making, the mixing and primary fermentation stages are the building blocks of flavor, structure, and complexity. The delicate interplay of ingredients, time, and fermentation allows the dough to transform from a simple mixture to a masterpiece of texture and taste. As the baker refines their techniques and develops a deep understanding of these critical steps, they embark on a journey of artisanal craftsmanship, crafting loaves that bear the distinctive qualities of true sourdough bread.

2.5 DOUGH DIVISION AND RESTING

Dough Division and Resting are crucial steps in the sourdough bread-making process that contribute to the final shape, texture, and flavor of the loaf. Each step requires precision, finesse, and a keen understanding of the dough's characteristics. Let us explore these steps in detail, unraveling the techniques that lead to beautifully formed loaves.

After the primary fermentation stage, the fully fermented dough is ready to be divided into individual portions that will eventually become individual loaves. Dividing is a crucial step in ensuring consistent loaf sizes and facilitating even fermentation.

The baker begins by gently transferring the dough onto a lightly floured work surface. Using a bench scraper or a dough cutter, the dough is divided into portions of equal weight. The exact weight may vary depending on the desired loaf size, but consistency is key to achieving uniform results.

During the dividing process, the baker handles the dough with care, mindful of preserving the gas bubbles created during fermentation. These gas bubbles contribute to the dough's structure and lightness, resulting in a well-risen and open crumb in the final loaf.

The divided portions of dough are then rounded or lightly shaped into individual balls. This process helps tighten the dough's surface and create tension, which is essential for achieving a well-shaped loaf during the final shaping stage. The rounded portions of dough are then allowed to rest briefly, usually for about 10 to 15 minutes, to relax and redistribute the gluten.

After the initial dividing, the dough undergoes preshaping—a gentle shaping process that prepares the dough for its final shape. Preshaping further strengthens the dough's structure, enhances its surface tension, and promotes proper fermentation during the bench rest.

To preshape the dough, the baker gently flattens each portion of dough into a rough rectangle or oval shape. They then fold the sides of the dough inward, overlapping them slightly at the center. This folding motion helps create tension on the dough's surface, further strengthening its structure.

The preshaped dough is then carefully flipped over, seam side down, and allowed to rest briefly on the work surface. This resting period, usually lasting about 10 to 15 minutes, allows the gluten to relax and makes the final shaping process more manageable.

The bench rest is a crucial stage that follows the preshaping process. During this resting period, the dough undergoes a final phase of fermentation, further developing its flavor, texture, and structure.

The preshaped dough is placed on the work surface, seam side down, and covered with a clean cloth or a lightly greased plastic wrap. It is essential to provide a warm and draft-free environment for the bench rest, typically at room temperature or slightly warmer.

The duration of the bench rest depends on various factors, such as dough hydration, ambient temperature, and desired flavor profile. Generally, the bench rest lasts between 20 minutes to 1 hour.

During this time, the dough continues to ferment, allowing the flavors to deepen and the gluten to relax further.

The bench rest also contributes to the dough's extensibility, making it easier to shape without tearing or damaging the gluten structure. It allows the dough to reach an optimal state for the final shaping, resulting in well-formed loaves with good volume and an even crumb structure.

Throughout the bench rest, the baker monitors the dough's progress, keeping an eye on signs of fermentation activity. The dough should visibly rise and increase in volume, becoming slightly puffy and airy.

After the bench rest, the dough is ready for the final shaping, where it takes on its distinctive loaf form. The shaping process varies depending on the desired loaf shape, whether it be boules (round loaves), batards (oval loaves), or other creative shapes. The shaping techniques involve carefully tucking and tightening the dough to create tension and structure.

In conclusion, the steps of dividing, preshaping, and bench rest are integral to the sourdough bread-making process. Each step contributes to the dough's structure, texture, and flavor, setting the stage for the final shaping and subsequent stages of proofing and baking. With patience, skill, and attention to detail, the baker ensures that the dough is in optimal condition, ready to transform into beautifully formed loaves that will bring delight to those who savor the art of sourdough bread.

2.6 LOAF MOLDING

Loaf molding is the process of giving the dough its final form and structure before it undergoes its final proofing and baking. It is a delicate and meticulous step that requires attention to detail, as it determines the loaf's appearance and crumb structure.

To begin the molding process, the baker gently transfers the dough onto a lightly floured work surface. The dough is usually in the form of a flattened round (if shaping a boule) or a rectangle (if shaping a batard). The baker carefully handles the dough, being mindful of preserving the gas bubbles formed during fermentation, as they contribute to the loaf's lightness and texture.

The goal of molding is to create tension on the dough's surface, which gives the loaf structure and enables it to hold its shape during the final proofing and baking. There are various shaping techniques, each suited to different loaf shapes and styles. Here, we'll explore the shaping process for a basic boule:

a. **Preshape**: The dough is gently folded from the edges towards the center to create tension and strengthen the gluten network. This helps to create a round shape and develop surface tension. The dough is then allowed to rest for a short period, typically 10 to 15 minutes, to relax the gluten and make it more pliable for the final shaping.

b. **Final shape**: After the brief rest, the baker carefully flips the dough over, seam side down, to ensure a smooth, rounded top surface. The edges of the dough are then gently folded towards the center, creating tension on the surface. This folding motion can be repeated several times until the desired shape and tension are achieved.

c. **Surface tightening**: The dough is further shaped by using the palm of the hand or fingertips to gently rotate and tuck the dough under itself in a circular motion. This action tightens the surface and helps to create a smooth, taut outer layer.

d. **Sealing**: Once the shaping is complete, the seam side of the dough is carefully sealed by pinching the edges together, ensuring a tight seal to maintain the shape during proofing and baking.

The molding process may vary depending on the desired loaf shape and personal preferences. Each shaping technique requires practice and a keen understanding of the dough's characteristics. It is important to handle the dough gently to avoid degassing or tearing, as this can affect the final crumb structure and oven spring.

2.7 DOUGH MATURATION

After shaping, the dough enters the dough maturation stage, where it undergoes its final fermentation, allowing it to rise and develop its flavor, texture, and structure. dough maturation is a crucial step that requires patience and careful monitoring to achieve optimal results.

During dough maturation, the shaped dough is placed in a suitable container or on a proofing surface, such as a proofing basket or a lined baking sheet. The dough needs to be protected from drying out, so it is usually covered with a cloth or placed in a food-grade plastic bag to create a warm and humid environment.

Dough maturation can take place at room temperature or in a slightly warmer environment, depending on the desired fermentation speed and flavor development. The duration of proofing can vary widely, ranging from a few hours to overnight, depending on factors such as dough hydration, ambient temperature, and desired flavor profile.

During the maturation stage, the dough undergoes a final fermentation as the wild yeast and bacteria in the sourdough culture continue to metabolize and produce carbon dioxide gas. This gas gets trapped in the dough, causing it to rise further and develop an airy, open crumb structure.

The baker monitors the proofing process closely, looking for visual cues to determine when the dough is adequately proofed. Signs of a well-proofed dough include increased volume, a slight jiggle when gently shaken, and a finger poke test that leaves a gentle indentation that springs back slowly.

However, it's important not to over-proof the dough, as it can result in a flat and dense loaf with less oven spring. Careful observation and experience are key to achieving the desired level of proofing. Adjustments can be made in subsequent bakes based on the observations made during the maturation stage.

The timing of the proofing process is influenced by various factors, including ambient temperature, dough temperature, and the strength of the sourdough culture. Bakers often develop a feel for the dough's readiness through practice and experience, allowing them to make informed judgments about when it is time to proceed to the next step.

It's worth noting that the maturation stage is not just about fermentation; it also allows the dough to relax and stabilize, making it easier to handle during the scoring and baking process. The gluten structure continues to develop and mature, contributing to a well-formed loaf with good volume and texture.

In conclusion, shaping and maturation are critical steps in the sourdough bread-making process. Through shaping, the dough takes on its final form, with tension and structure that will contribute to a well-risen loaf. During proofing, the dough undergoes its final fermentation, allowing the flavors to deepen, the crumb structure to develop, and the loaf to achieve its desired characteristics. With practice, observation, and an understanding of the dough's behavior, bakers can master these steps and create beautifully shaped and proofed sourdough loaves that are a testament to their skill and craftsmanship.

2.8 DECORATIVE SLITS

Decorative Slits in sourdough bread-making is the technique of making shallow cuts or slashes on the surface of the dough just before baking. It serves both functional and aesthetic purposes. Functionally, scoring helps control the oven spring, allowing the dough to expand evenly during baking. The cuts create weak points that guide the dough's rise and prevent it from bursting or cracking in unintended areas. This controlled expansion promotes an open crumb structure and ensures a visually appealing loaf.

Decorative Slits also aids in gas release, allowing trapped gases to escape from the dough. It prevents an explosion of the dough and ensures a more even texture throughout the bread. Additionally, the cuts on the dough's surface promote crust development by exposing it directly to the oven's heat. This results in a crisp and well-colored crust, adding to the overall sensory experience of the bread.

From an aesthetic standpoint, decorative slits offers bakers the opportunity to express their creativity and leave a unique mark on their loaves. Different scoring patterns, such as single slashes, parallel lines, or intricate designs, can be used to create visually appealing patterns on the bread's surface. These patterns not only enhance the bread's appearance but also serve as a distinctive identifier for bakers, reflecting their craftsmanship and personal style.

To achieve effective scoring, bakers should use a sharp blade to make clean and precise cuts. The angle and depth of the cuts are important considerations, with a 30 to 45-degree angle generally recommended. Timing is crucial, with scoring done just before baking when the dough's surface is slightly firm but still flexible. By experimenting with different scoring techniques, patterns, and depths, bakers can develop their own unique styles and elevate their sourdough bread-making skills.

In summary, decorative slits plays a vital role in sourdough bread-making. It helps control the dough's expansion, ensures gas release, promotes crust development, and allows bakers to showcase their creativity. With careful consideration of techniques and artistic choices, scoring contributes to both the functionality and beauty of the final sourdough loaf.

2.9 BAKING

The baking step in the sourdough bread-making process is the culmination of careful preparation and precise execution. It is the stage where the shaped and proofed dough transforms into a beautifully golden and fragrant loaf. Baking involves the application of heat to the dough, causing it to undergo various physical and chemical changes that result in a flavorful crust and a well-developed crumb

Before placing the dough in the oven, it is crucial to preheat the oven to the desired temperature. The temperature depends on the recipe and the desired crust color and texture. Most sourdough recipes recommend preheating the oven to a high temperature, usually between 425°F (220°C) and 475°F (245°C). Preheating the oven ensures that the dough receives immediate heat, promoting proper oven spring and crust formation.

Steam plays a vital role in the baking of sourdough bread. The presence of steam in the early stages of baking helps create a crisp and glossy crust while allowing the dough to expand to its fullest potential. Steam keeps the surface of the dough moist, allowing it to stretch and rise before the crust sets.

To introduce steam into the oven, bakers employ various methods. One common technique is to place a pan of hot water in the oven while preheating to create a steam-rich environment. Another method involves spritzing the dough with water just before placing it in the oven or using a spray bottle to mist the oven walls to create a burst of steam.

During the initial phase of baking, a phenomenon known as oven spring occurs. As the dough is exposed to the heat of the oven, the trapped carbon dioxide gas rapidly expands, causing the loaf to rise and take on its final shape. This rapid expansion is a result of the yeast's and bacteria's continued fermentation and the heat-induced expansion of the gases within the dough.

Oven spring is influenced by several factors, including the dough's fermentation activity, gluten strength, and oven temperature. A well-fermented dough with a robust gluten structure and an adequately hot oven will typically experience a satisfying oven spring, resulting in a loaf with good volume and an open crumb.

As the baking process progresses, the surface of the dough undergoes a series of transformations that lead to the development of a crust. The Maillard reaction, a chemical reaction between amino acids and reducing sugars in the dough, occurs during baking, resulting in the browning of the crust and the generation of complex flavors.

The crust's texture and color can be influenced by various factors, such as oven temperature, steam presence, and the dough's hydration level. A higher oven temperature and the initial presence of steam contribute to a crust with a deep golden color and a crisp texture.

Monitoring the internal temperature of the loaf is crucial for ensuring that the bread is thoroughly baked. The desired internal temperature for most sourdough bread is around 200°F (93°C) to 210°F (99°C). A reliable instant-read thermometer inserted into the thickest part of the loaf helps determine whether the bread has reached the desired temperature.

Achieving the correct internal temperature ensures that the crumb is fully cooked, without any doughy or underbaked sections. It also helps prevent a gummy or overly dense crumb texture.

Once the bread has reached the desired internal temperature and achieved a beautifully golden crust, it is important to allow it to cool properly before slicing. Cooling allows the residual moisture within the crumb to redistribute, ensuring an even and moist crumb texture. It also helps the crust to fully set, resulting in a satisfying crunch.

During the cooling process, it is recommended to place the bread on a wire rack to allow air circulation around the loaf, preventing condensation and maintaining the crust's integrity.

In conclusion, the baking step in sourdough bread-making is a critical stage where the shaped and proofed dough transforms into a fragrant and visually appealing loaf. Through preheating, steam generation, oven spring, crust formation, monitoring the internal temperature, and proper cooling, the baker ensures that the bread develops a flavorful crust, a well-developed crumb, and an enticing aroma. Mastering the art of baking sourdough bread requires practice, keen observation, and an understanding of the dough's behavior. With each bake, the baker hones their skills, striving to create the perfect loaf that showcases the best of sourdough craftsmanship.

2.10 PRESENTATION AND PRESERVATION

Serving is the final stage of the sourdough bread-making process, where the freshly baked bread is prepared for consumption

Once the sourdough bread is baked, it should be allowed to cool completely on a wire rack. This process is crucial as it helps set the crumb structure and prevents moisture buildup inside the loaf.

After the bread has cooled down, it can be sliced according to personal preference. Sourdough bread has a firm crust and a moist, airy crumb, making it suitable for various types of slicing, such as thin slices for sandwiches or thicker slices for toast.

If the bread is not consumed immediately, it should be stored properly to maintain its freshness. Wrapping the bread in a clean cloth or placing it in a bread box can help retain its texture and prevent it from drying out. For an appealing presentation, you can place the bread on a wooden board or a decorative bread basket.

Proper storage of sourdough bread is essential to maintain its quality and freshness over an extended period.

Before storing the bread, ensure that it has cooled down completely. If warm bread is stored, it can create a humid environment, leading to mold growth.

To prevent the bread from drying out, it should be wrapped tightly in a breathable material like wax paper or parchment paper. Avoid using plastic bags as they can trap moisture and make the crust soggy.

Sourdough bread can be stored at room temperature for 2-3 days. However, it is important to note that the bread's shelf life can vary depending on the specific recipe and environmental conditions. To extend its freshness, you can consider freezing the bread.

Sourdough bread freezes exceptionally well. Slice the bread if desired, and wrap each slice or the entire loaf tightly in plastic wrap or aluminum foil. Place the wrapped bread in a freezer bag to protect it from freezer burn. Properly stored, sourdough bread can remain fresh in the freezer for up to three months.

When you're ready to enjoy the frozen sourdough bread, remove the desired number of slices or the entire loaf from the freezer. Allow them to thaw at room temperature, or for a faster thaw, use a toaster or an oven set to a low temperature.

The cleanup phase involves tidying up the kitchen and equipment used during the sourdough bread-making process

Start by cleaning the utensils and equipment used, such as mixing bowls, measuring cups, spoons, and any dough scrapers or bench scrapers. Remove any dough residue by scraping it off with a dough scraper and then wash the items with warm soapy water. Rinse thoroughly and dry them properly before storing.

Clean the countertop or any other work surface used for kneading and shaping the dough. Remove any dough scraps or flour residues, and wipe the surface with a damp cloth or sponge. Use a mild detergent if necessary, and ensure the surface is thoroughly clean and dry.

If you used baking sheets or pans during the bread-making process, clean them thoroughly. Remove any stuck-on dough or burnt bits by soaking the pans in warm soapy water. Scrub them gently with a non-abrasive sponge or brush to avoid damaging the non-stick coating, if applicable. Rinse the pans and dry them properly before storing.

If any dough or flour spills occurred in the oven during baking, it's important to clean them up to prevent smoke or odors in future baking endeavors. Allow the oven to cool completely, then remove any loose debris with a brush or cloth. Use an oven cleaner or a mixture of baking soda and water to tackle any stubborn stains or residue. Follow the manufacturer's instructions for oven cleaning products and ensure proper ventilation while cleaning.

Once all the specific areas are cleaned, give the kitchen a final cleanup. Wipe down the countertops, sweep the floor, and dispose of any leftover ingredients or packaging. Return all utensils, equipment, and ingredients to their designated places for easy access the next time you bake sourdough bread.

In conclusion, serving, storage, and cleanup are essential steps in the sourdough bread-making process. By following these steps carefully, you can enjoy freshly baked sourdough bread, preserve its quality, and maintain a clean and organized kitchen

2.11 BAKER'S MATH

Baker's percentages, also known as baker's formula or baker's math, are a fundamental tool in the world of bread-making. They provide a standardized method for expressing the ingredient proportions in a bread recipe based on the weight of flour. Baker's percentages are a common tool used in the baking world to scale recipes, achieve consistent results, and have precise control over the fermentation and hydration levels of their dough.

At the core of baker's percentages is the concept of flour as the benchmark, represented as 100%. All other ingredients in the recipe are then expressed as a percentage of the mass of flour. This allows bakers to calculate ingredient amounts accurately and make adjustments depending on their desired outcomes.

Water is a key ingredient in bread-making, and its percentage in a recipe plays a crucial role in determining the dough's hydration level. The water percentage is typically higher in sourdough bread recipes compared to traditional bread recipes. Higher hydration levels, ranging from 60% to 85% or more, result in a wetter and more extensible dough, leading to larger air pockets and an open crumb structure.

Sourdough bread is characterized by its unique tangy flavor, which comes from the fermentation of a sourdough starter. The sourdough starter, fermentation product made from flour and water using natural yeast and lactobacilli bacteria, is added to the recipe as a percentage of the flour weight. The percentage of sourdough starter used can vary depending on factors such as desired fermentation time and the level of sourness desired in the final bread. Common percentages range from 10% to 30%.Salt, another crucial ingredient, is added to bread dough for flavor enhancement and to regulate the fermentation process. It controls the activity of yeast and bacteria, slows down fermentation, and strengthens the gluten structure. Salt is typically added as a percentage of the flour weight and commonly ranges from 2% to 3%.Other ingredients, such as olive oil, honey, herbs, seeds, or nuts, can be incorporated into sourdough bread recipes to add complexity and variation. These ingredients are added in smaller quantities, and their percentages are calculated based on the flour weight. The percentages of these additional ingredients can vary depending on the specific recipe and desired flavors.

Baker's percentages offer several benefits to bakers. They provide consistency, allowing bakers to replicate the same results each time they bake a particular recipe. The percentages also facilitate recipe scaling, enabling bakers to adjust ingredient amounts for different batch sizes while maintaining the same ratios. Baker's percentages are valuable tools for recipe development and experimentation, as they allow bakers to precisely adjust ingredient proportions to achieve specific characteristics in their bread, such as crumb texture, crust thickness, or flavor intensity.

Moreover, baker's percentages aid in troubleshooting bread-making issues. By analyzing the ratios of ingredients in a recipe, bakers can identify potential problem areas and make adjustments accordingly.

In conclusion, baker's percentages are an essential aspect of sourdough bread-making. They provide a standardized and scalable method for expressing ingredient proportions based on the weight of flour. By utilizing baker's percentages, bakers can achieve consistent results, have precise control over hydration and fermentation levels, and unleash their creativity in the art of sourdough bread-making.

2.12 AUTOLYSE

Autolyse is a vital step in the process of manufacturing sourdough bread. It is a period of rest during which the flour and water are mixed together and permitted to hydrate before the addition of salt and additional mixing or kneading. While autolyse may seem like a little and simple procedure, it plays a vital part in producing the texture, flavor, and overall quality of the final bread.

During autolyse, the flour and water come together to produce a cohesive combination. The goal of this step is to allow the flour to absorb the water fully and initiate the gluten formation process. Gluten, a complex protein network, is crucial for giving bread its structure and flexibility. When flour comes into touch with water, two proteins found in wheat flour, gliadin, and glutenin, combine to form gluten.

The hydration time of autolyse allows the flour particles to absorb water equally, resulting in a more consistent and thorough hydration of the dough. This hydration process activates enzymes present in the flour, principally amylase and protease. Amylase breaks down starches into simpler sugars, giving sustenance for the yeast during fermentation. Protease, on the other hand, contributes to the breakdown of proteins, which helps in the production of a softer crumb.

Autolyse also contributes in gluten formation. As the flour hydrates, the glutenin proteins absorb water and begin a process termed hydration-induced protein unfolding. This unfolding allows the glutenin proteins to interact with one another, forming a network that gives the dough its strength and structure. This initial gluten synthesis during autolyse makes future kneading or mixing more successful in generating a strong gluten network.

The time of autolyse might vary depending on personal choice and recipe. Some bakers opt for a brief autolyse of 20 to 30 minutes, while others prefer a longer rest of many hours. A longer autolyse allows for more extensive gluten formation and can contribute to a more open and airy crumb in the final bread. However, it's vital not to exceed the ideal autolyse time, as the dough can become over-hydrated and difficult to manage.

One of the primary benefits of autolyse is greater dough extensibility. During the rest time, the gluten network continues to expand, becoming more elastic and easier to stretch and shape. This flexibility is particularly useful when it comes to moulding the dough into loaves or other desired forms. It allows the baker to obtain a well-defined shape and structure without excessive resistance from the dough.

Autolyse also adds to better flavor development in sourdough bread. The enzymes activated during this time break down complex carbs and proteins into simpler forms, releasing natural sugars and amino acids. These components contribute to the overall taste and scent of the final bread, providing depth and richness to its flavor profile.

While autolyse is a useful phase in the sourdough bread-making process, it is crucial to note that it is not a mandatory step. Some bakers choose to skip autolyse and continue directly to the mixing or kneading stage. However, including autolyse into your bread-making routine can lead to enhanced dough handling, texture, and flavor

CHAPTER 3
TROUBLESHOOTING

Troubleshooting Common Issues in Sourdough Bread Making

3.1 SOURDOUGH STARTER

Creating and maintaining a sourdough starter can be a lengthy process. It's normal for a starter to lose its initial activity within 5 to 7 days after creation. However, don't be discouraged, as it takes time to develop a healthy and robust starter with a distinct sour taste. It may take months or even years to achieve, but you should be able to bake a loaf within a month.

3.2 TEMPERATURE OF THE ROOM AND SOURDOUGH CULTURE

The ambient room temperature affects the activity of your sourdough starter. Cooler temperatures can slow down its growth, while warmer temperatures can make it overactive, resulting in a less pronounced sour flavor. If you bake frequently, experiment with different spots in your house to find the ideal temperature for your starter. A happy and active starter should rise within 5 to 8 hours after feeding. If you bake less often, store your starter in the fridge and feed it a couple of times before baking.

3.3 AMBIENT TEMPERATURE AND DOUGH RISING

The ambient temperature also plays a significant role in the rising of your sourdough dough. Cooler or drafty environments will slow down the rising process, while warmer and draft-free areas facilitate faster fermentation. Additionally, using ingredients like eggs, milk, butter, or their vegan alternatives at colder temperatures can further impede the rising of your bread. Ensure that your dough is placed in a relatively warm and draft-free spot to optimize the fermentation process. For enriched dough, using room-temperature ingredients will help speed up the rising.

3.4 ALTERNATIVES TO REFINED FLOUR AND WHOLE GRAINS

In most recipes, you can substitute up to half of the plain flour with whole wheat flour. Although working with whole wheat flour can be more challenging, it adds nutritional value to your bread. If you're experienced, you can experiment with modifying your favorite recipes to incorporate whole grains.

3.5 PROOFING

Proofing is the final rising phase before baking your sourdough bread. Proper proofing is crucial for achieving desirable results.

3.6 UNDER-PROOFED SOURDOUGH

Insufficient proofing time can lead to an under-proofed loaf. Signs of under-proofed sourdough include a "tight" crumb instead of an open and airy texture, possible gumminess and density when sliced, and the likelihood of large empty air pockets inside the loaf. Allow adequate time for proofing to ensure optimal texture and flavor.

3.7 STICKINESS & STICKING

Sourdough bread dough tends to be sticky, making handling a bit challenging. To reduce sticking, lightly wet your fingers or hands with water instead of using flour. If your shaped loaves stick to the banneton or bowl, dusting them with regular or rice flour before placing the dough inside can help. Alternatively, you can line the banneton or bowl with a clean cotton kitchen towel. A slight build-up of flour residue over time can reduce sticking.

3.8 SCORING & SLASHING

Achieving clean decorative cuts on the top of your loaf requires attention to a few factors.

3.9 INADEQUATE TENSION AND SHAPING

If your bread's outer surface is slack and lacks tension, your scoring may not result in clean cuts. Pay attention to shaping techniques to ensure proper tension and structure in the dough.

3.10 DULL CUTTING BLADE

Using a dull lame or cutting blade can make it difficult to achieve clean slashes. Regularly replace your blades to maintain sharpness for clean scoring.

3.11 INSUFFICIENT SCORING DEPTH

Ensure that you score the dough deep enough. A clean score should be clearly visible without the dough attempting to reconnect.

By addressing these common troubleshooting points, you'll be better equipped to overcome challenges and achieve excellent results in your sourdough bread-making journey.

CHAPTER 4
NUTRITION AND HEALTH BENEFITS

In this chapter, we will delve into the nutrition and health benefits of sourdough bread. From enhanced digestibility to improved nutrient bioavailability and gut health, sourdough offers a range of advantages that make it a nourishing choice for individuals seeking a wholesome and delicious bread option.

4.1 ENHANCED DIGESTIBILITY AND GUT HEALTH

Sourdough bread's fermentation process sets it apart from other bread types, making it easier to digest for many individuals. During fermentation, beneficial bacteria and yeast present in the sourdough starter break down complex carbohydrates and gluten. This breakdown of complex carbohydrates into simpler forms can alleviate digestive discomfort for those with sensitivities or intolerances.

Moreover, sourdough's fermentation introduces lactic acid bacteria, which can promote a healthy gut microbiome. These bacteria produce lactic acid, creating an acidic environment that inhibits the growth of harmful bacteria while encouraging the proliferation of beneficial gut bacteria. A balanced and diverse gut microbiome is crucial for optimal digestion, nutrient absorption, and overall well-being.

4.2 IMPROVED NUTRIENT BIOAVAILABILITY

Sourdough bread offers improved nutrient bioavailability compared to bread made with commercial yeast. Grains naturally contain phytic acid, which can bind to minerals like iron, zinc, and calcium, inhibiting their absorption in the body. However, the fermentation process in sourdough activates enzymes that break down phytic acid, releasing these essential minerals and making them more accessible for absorption.

The reduction of phytic acid through fermentation not only enhances mineral absorption but also unlocks the potential of other nutrients present in sourdough. B-vitamins, such as thiamin, riboflavin, niacin, and folate, become more bioavailable in sourdough bread, supporting various bodily functions, including energy metabolism and red blood cell production.

4.3 LOW GLYCEMIC INDEX AND BLOOD SUGAR REGULATION

Sourdough bread has a lower glycemic index (GI) compared to bread made with commercial yeast. The glycemic index measures how quickly a food raises blood sugar levels. The slow fermentation process in sourdough leads to the production of organic acids and other compounds that slow down the digestion and absorption of carbohydrates.

As a result, sourdough bread causes a more gradual and moderate increase in blood glucose levels compared to bread made with conventional yeast. The gradual release of glucose into the bloodstream aids in glucose monitoring and blood sugar control and provides a sustained release of energy, promoting satiety and reducing the risk of blood sugar spikes and crashes. This makes sourdough bread a favorable option for individuals with diabetes or those aiming to manage their blood sugar levels.

4.4 RICH IN BENEFICIAL NUTRIENTS

Sourdough bread is not only delicious but also nutrient-dense. It contains an array of essential nutrients that support overall health and well-being. B-vitamins, such as thiamin, riboflavin, niacin, and folate, play crucial roles in energy production, cellular function, and the maintenance of a healthy nervous system.

Additionally, sourdough bread provides minerals like iron, zinc, magnesium, and selenium, which are essential for various bodily functions, including immune function, bone health, and antioxidant defense. These nutrients are naturally present in the grains used to make sourdough bread and become more bioavailable through the fermentation process, ensuring optimal nutrient utilization by the body.

4.5 PREBIOTIC AND PROBIOTIC PROPERTIES

Sourdough bread exhibits both prebiotic and probiotic properties, contributing to a healthy gut environment. Prebiotics are non-digestible fibers that serve as food for beneficial gut bacteria, promoting their growth and activity. Sourdough bread contains prebiotic compounds, such as fructans and other fermentable fibers that nourish the gut microbiota.

Furthermore, the fermentation process introduces lactic acid bacteria into the dough, acting as probiotics. These live bacteria can confer health benefits when consumed, such as improving digestion, supporting the immune system, and reducing inflammation. By incorporating sourdough bread into your diet, you can support a balanced and diverse gut microbiome, which is associated with various aspects of health.

4.6 REDUCED PRESERVATIVES AND ADDITIVES

Sourdough bread is often made using simple, natural ingredients, without the need for preservatives, artificial flavors, or additives. Unlike commercially produced bread, which may contain these additives to extend shelf life or enhance flavor, sourdough relies on the natural fermentation process for preservation and flavor development.

By choosing sourdough bread, you can reduce your exposure to potentially harmful additives and enjoy a more wholesome and natural bread option that aligns with a healthy lifestyle.

Sourdough bread offers a myriad of nutrition and health benefits. Its enhanced digestibility, improved nutrient bioavailability, low glycemic index, and rich nutrient profile make it a valuable addition to a balanced diet. Additionally, it's prebiotic and probiotic properties, along with the absence of preservatives and additives, further contribute to its health-promoting qualities. Embrace the art of sourdough and enjoy its delicious taste while reaping the nutritional benefits it has to offer for your overall well-being.

CHAPTER 5
BASIC SOURDOUGH BREAD RECIPES

1. CLASSIC LOAF

Prep Time: 30 minutes

Total Time: 48-72 hours (including fermentation and proofing time)

Serving: 1 loaf

INGREDIENTS

- 4 cups high-quality bread flour
- 2 and a half cups active sourdough starter (prepared with your preferred feeding routine)
- 1.5 cups water (at room temperature)
- Pinch of sea salt

DIRECTIONS

1. Get ready to embark on a delightful bread-making adventure! Measure your flour meticulously or use the classic spoon-and-sweep method to fill a cup, removing any excess. Blend all the ingredients together, and let the magic of mixing and kneading unfold. Whether you prefer the tactile experience of kneading by hand, the convenience of a mixer, or the assistance of a trusty bread machine, spend some quality time shaping a soft and smooth dough. The time required may vary, but the rhythmic motion and anticipation will make it an enjoyable journey.

2. Allow the dough to take a breather in a cozy, lightly greased bowl. This is its time to rise and shine, getting puffy and full of character. Give it around 45 to 60 minutes to show off its progress, reaching a puffy state that might not necessarily double in size but is undeniably promising.

3. Picture a 9" x 5" loaf pan eagerly waiting to be part of this bread extravaganza. Lightly grease it, offering a hospitable environment for the dough to settle into its destined shape.

4. Here's where the real transformation happens! Gently deflate the dough, as if whispering encouraging words, and start shaping it into a magnificent 9" log. Witness the dough's pliability as it cooperatively takes on this new form. Nestle the log into the prepared pan, cover it, and let it rise for 60 to 90 minutes. Watch with anticipation as it stretches upward, cresting about an inch over the rim of the pan, almost as if it's showing off its rising prowess.

5. As the excitement builds, preheat the oven to 350°F. The stage is set for the bread to reveal its true colors.

6. It's time to let the bread bask in the oven's warm embrace. Bake it for 40 to 50 minutes, eagerly observing its transformation into a light golden masterpiece. To ensure its readiness, employ a trusty digital thermometer, gently inserting it into the center. When it reaches a temperature of 190°F, you'll know it has reached its desired internal perfection.

7. The grand finale! As the bread emerges from the oven, let it revel in its glory for a couple of minutes. Then, with a gentle flourish, release it from the pan onto a cooling rack. The aroma and sight of freshly baked bread will enchant you as it cools, preparing for its moment to shine. Feel free to slice into it or engage your senses by savoring the anticipation a little longer.

8. Remember, this bread has a story to tell. It can keep you company for several delightful days when stored at room temperature, lovingly wrapped. If you desire an extended journey, embrace the art of preservation and freeze it for longer-lasting enjoyment.

Nutrition Value (per serving): Calories: 160 calories; Proteins: 6 grams; Carbs: 35 grams; Fats: 1 gram; Cholesterol: 0 milligrams; Sodium: 500 milligrams

2. CINNAMON ROLLS

Prep Time: 30 minutes   **Total Time:** 3 hours 30 minutes   **Servings:** 12 rolls

INGREDIENTS

- 1 cup active sourdough starter
- 1 cup milk
- 4 cups flour
- 1/4 cup granulated sugar
- 1/4 cup unsalted butter, melted
- 2 teaspoons ground cinnamon
- 1/2 teaspoon salt
- 1/2 tsp. baking soda
- 1/2 cup brown sugar
- 1/4 cup unsalted butter
- 1 cup powdered sugar
- 2 tablespoons milk
- 1/2 teaspoon vanilla extract

DIRECTIONS

1. In a mixing bowl, combine the active sourdough starter and milk. Stir in the flour, granulated sugar, melted butter, cinnamon, and salt until a dough forms.
2. Knead the dough on a lightly floured surface for about 5 minutes until elastic and smooth. Place the dough in a greased bowl, cover, and let it rise for 2 hours.
3. After the dough has risen, punch it down and roll it out into a rectangle. Spread the softened butter over the dough and sprinkle with brown sugar.
4. Roll up the dough tightly from the long side to form a log. Cut the log into 12 equal-sized rolls and place them in a greased baking dish. Cover and let them rise for another 1 hour.
5. Preheat the oven to 375°F (190°C). In a small bowl, mix the baking soda with 1 tablespoon of water and brush it over the risen rolls.
6. Bake the cinnamon rolls for 20-25 minutes until golden brown. Meanwhile, prepare the glaze by whisking together powdered sugar, milk, as well as vanilla essence.
7. Remove the rolls out of your oven let them cool for a few minutes before drizzling the glaze over the top. Serve warm and enjoy!

Nutrition Value (per serving): Calories: 297; Proteins: 5g; Carbs: 54g; Fats: 7g; Cholesterol: 15mg; Sodium: 205mg

3. BAGUETTES

Prep Time: 40 minutes   **Total Time:** 24 hours   **Serving:** 2 baguettes

INGREDIENTS

- 4 cups bread flour
- 1.5 cups water(room temperature)
- 2 cups active sourdough starter
- Pinch of salt

DIRECTIONS

1. Bread flour and water should be mixed together in a big bowl. Whisk until the mixture forms rough, uneven dough. Cover the bowl and let it rest for 30 minutes.
2. Add the active sourdough starter to the bowl and mix it into the dough. Let it rest for 10 minutes.
3. Sprinkle the salt over the dough and knead it for about 10-15 minutes until the dough is elastic and smooth.
4. Place the dough back into the bowl, cover it, and let it rise at room temperature for about 3-4 hours till it was twice as big.
5. Preheat the oven to 450°F (230°C). Place a baking stone or baking sheet in the oven to preheat as well.
6. Divide the risen dough into two equal portions. Shape each portion into a baguette by rolling it tightly and tapering the ends.
7. Place the baguettes onto the preheated baking stone or sheet. Score the tops of the baguettes diagonally with a sharp knife.
8. Bake for 25-30 minutes until the baguettes are golden brown and have a crisp crust. Remove out of your oven let them cool on a wire rack before slicing.

Nutrition Values (per serving): Calories: 180; Proteins: 6g; Carbs: 38g; Fats: 1g; Cholesterol: 0mg; Sodium: 400mg

4. BANANA BREAD

Prep Time: 15 minutes   **Total Time:** 1 hour 15 minutes   **Servings:** 12 slices

INGREDIENTS

- 1 cup sourdough discard
- A half-cup of unsalted butter
- 1 cup granulated sugar
- 2 large eggs
- 3 ripe bananas, mashed
- 1 tsp. vanilla extract
- 2 cups flour
- 1 tsp. baking soda
- 1/2 teaspoon salt

DIRECTIONS

1. Preheat the oven to 350°F (175°C). Grease a 9x5-inch loaf pan and set it aside.
2. In a mixing bowl, combine the sourdough discard, melted butter, and sugar. Add the eggs, mashed bananas, as well as vanilla essence, and mix well.
3. In a separate bowl, whip together the flour, baking soda, and salt. Gradually add the dry ingredients to the wet ingredients, stirring until just combined.
4. Pour the batter into the prepared loaf pan and smooth the top. Bake for 60-70 minutes or when a toothpick is put into the center arrives clear.
5. Remove the banana bread out of your oven let it cool in the pan for 10 minutes. Then transfer it to a wire rack to cool completely before slicing and serving.

Nutrition Value (per serving): Calories: 256; Proteins: 4g; Carbs: 41g; Fats: 9g; Cholesterol: 52mg; Sodium: 246mg

CHAPTER 6
ARTISAN BASIC SOURDOUGH BREADS

1. BASIC BREAD

Prep Time: 30 minutes   **Total Time:** 2 hours, 20 minutes   **Servings:** 2

INGREDIENTS

- 1 ½ cups warm water
- 1 ½ teaspoons active dry yeast (equivalent to half a packet)
- 2 teaspoons sugar
- 3 cups all-purpose flour
- 1 ½ teaspoons salt

DIRECTIONS

1. In a large mixing bowl or stand mixer, combine the warm water, active dry yeast, and sugar. Allow the mixture to sit for approximately 10 minutes until it becomes bubbly and activates the yeast.
2. Add the all-purpose flour and salt to the bowl. Mix thoroughly until all the ingredients are well combined, resulting in a soft dough. The dough should have a slightly sticky consistency, but manageable. If the dough is too sticky, gradually add small amounts of flour (about 1 tablespoon at a time) until it reaches the desired texture.
3. Loosely cover the bowl with plastic wrap and a kitchen towel. Let the dough rise for a period of 1 to 3 hours, allowing it to develop a richer flavor over a longer rise time.
4. Preheat the oven to 450°F (230°C). Place a pizza stone or a flipped-over cookie sheet in the oven to preheat along with it.
5. Fill a baking dish with approximately 2 inches of water and place it on the bottom rack of the oven. This will create steam during baking and contribute to a crispy crust.
6. Sprinkle a small amount of flour on the countertop. Gently transfer the dough from the bowl onto the floured surface. Fold the dough onto itself a few times to enhance its structure. Divide the dough into two equal portions and shape each portion into a ball. Avoid excessive kneading or handling of the dough. If necessary, lightly dust the dough with flour to prevent sticking.
7. Use a sharp knife to make an X-shaped cut on the top of each dough ball. This helps the bread expand during baking.
8. Place the dough balls on a lightly floured pan and carefully transfer them onto the preheated pizza stone or cookie sheet.
9. Bake the bread for approximately 25 to 30 minutes or until it turns golden brown and is thoroughly cooked. The internal temperature of the bread should reach about 190°F (88°C) for optimal doneness.
10. Once baked, remove the bread out of your oven allow it to cool slightly on a wire rack before slicing and serving.
11. Enjoy the delightful experience of homemade artisan bread with its crusty exterior and tender interior!

Nutrition Value (per serving): Calories: 1412; Fat: 2g; Carbohydrates: 296g; Protein: 39g; Cholesterol: 0mg; Sodium: 2199mg

2. COUNTRY CRUST SOURDOUGH

Prep Time: 30 minutes   **Total Time:** 24 hours   **Serving:** 1 loaf

INGREDIENTS

- 4 cups bread flour
- 1.5 cups water (room temperature)
- 2 cups active sourdough starter
- Pinch of salt

DIRECTIONS

1. Bread flour and water should be mixed together in a big bowl. Whisk until the mixture forms rough, uneven dough. Cover the bowl with a clean kitchen towel and let it rest for 30 minutes.
2. After the autolyse, add the active sourdough starter to the bowl. Mix it into the dough using your hands or a spatula until well incorporated.
3. Sprinkle the salt over the dough and knead it for about 10-15 minutes until the dough becomes elastic and smooth.
4. Place the dough back into the bowl and cover it. Allow it to rise at room temperature for about 3-4 hours until it has size has more than doubled.
5. Preheat the oven to 450°F (230°C). Place a Dutch oven or a covered baking dish in the oven to preheat as well.
6. Carefully transfer the risen dough into the preheated Dutch oven. Score the top of the dough with a sharp knife.
7. Cover the Dutch oven and bake for 30 minutes. Then, remove the lid and bake for an additional 15-20 minutes until the crust is golden brown.
8. Remove the bread out of your oven let it cool on a wire rack before slicing.

Nutrition Values (per serving): Calories: 200; Proteins: 7g; Carbs: 42g; Fats: 1g; Cholesterol: 0mg; Sodium: 400mg

3. HERITAGE GRAIN ARTISAN SOURDOUGH

Prep Time: 45 minutes   **Total Time:** 24 hours   **Serving:** 1 loaf

INGREDIENTS

- 2 cups bread flour
- 1 cup whole wheat flour
- 1 cup spelt flour
- 1 and half cup water (room temperature)
- 1 and half cup active sourdough starter
- Pinch of salt

DIRECTIONS

1. In a large mixing bowl, combine the bread flour, whole wheat flour, spelt flour, and water. Stir until the mixture forms a shaggy dough. Cover the bowl and let it rest for 30 minutes.
2. Add the active sourdough starter to the bowl and mix it into the dough. Let it rest for 10 minutes.
3. Sprinkle the salt over the dough and knead it for about 10-15 minutes until the dough is elastic and smooth.
4. Place the dough back into the bowl, cover it, and let it rise at room temperature for about 3-4 hours until size has more than doubled.
5. Preheat the oven to 450°F (230°C). Place a Dutch oven or a covered baking dish in the oven to preheat as well.
6. Carefully transfer the risen dough into the preheated Dutch oven. Score the top of the dough with a sharp knife.
7. Cover the Dutch oven and bake for 30 minutes. Then, remove the lid and bake for an additional 15-20 minutes until the crust is golden brown.
8. Remove the bread out of your oven let it cool on a wire rack before slicing.

Nutrition Values (per serving): Calories: 190; Proteins: 6g; Carbs: 40g; Fats: 1g; Cholesterol: 0mg; Sodium: 400mg

4. OLIVE AND ROSEMARY BREAD

Prep Time: 20 minutes   **Total Time:** 4 hours 30 minutes   **Serving:** 1 loaf

INGREDIENTS

- 1 cup sourdough starter
- 2 1/2 cups bread flour
- 1/2 cup whole wheat flour
- 1 1/2 teaspoons salt
- 1 tablespoon chopped fresh rosemary
- 1/2 cup pitted olives, chopped
- 1 1/4 cups warm water

DIRECTIONS

1. In a large mixing bowl, combine the sourdough starter, bread flour, whole wheat flour, salt, chopped rosemary, and chopped olives.
2. Gradually add the warm water to the mixture, stirring until a shaggy dough forms.
3. Turn the dough out onto a board that has been lightly dusted with flour and knead for about 10 minutes, until elastic and smooth.
4. Place the dough in a greased bowl, cover with a clean kitchen towel, and let it rise in a warm place for about 3-4 hours, or until size has more than doubled.
5. Preheat the oven to 450°F (230°C). Place a Dutch oven or oven-safe pot with a lid in the oven while it preheats.
6. Carefully remove the hot pot out of your oven transfer the risen dough into it. Score the top of the dough with a sharp knife.
7. Cover the pot with the lid and bake for 30 minutes.
8. Remove the lid and continue baking for an additional 15-20 minutes, or until the bread is golden brown.
9. Remove the bread from the pot and let it cool completely on a wire rack before slicing.

Nutrition Value (per serving): Calories: 200; Proteins: 7g; Carbs: 40g; Fats: 2g; Cholesterol: 0mg; Sodium: 400mg

5. CRANBERRY WALNUT SOURDOUGH

Prep Time: 45 minutes   **Total Time:** 24 hours   **Serving:** 1 loaf

INGREDIENTS

- 3 and a half cup bread flour
- 1 cup whole wheat flour
- 1.5 cups water (room temperature)
- 1 and a half cup active sourdough starter
- Pinch of salt
- 1/2 cup dried cranberries
- 1/2 cup walnuts, chopped

DIRECTIONS

1. In a large mixing bowl, combine the bread flour, whole wheat flour, and water. Stir until the mixture forms a shaggy dough. Cover the bowl and let it rest for 30 minutes.
2. Add the active sourdough starter to the bowl and mix it into the dough. Let it rest for 10 minutes.
3. Sprinkle the salt over the dough and knead it for about 10-15 minutes until the dough is elastic and smooth.
4. Add the dried cranberries and chopped walnuts to the dough and knead for an additional 5 minutes to incorporate them evenly.
5. Place the dough back into the bowl, cover it, and let it rise at room temperature for about 3-4 hours till it was twice as big.
6. Preheat the oven to 450°F (230°C). Place a Dutch oven or a covered baking dish in the oven to preheat as well.
7. Carefully transfer the risen dough into the preheated Dutch oven. Score the top of the dough with a sharp knife.
8. Cover the Dutch oven and bake for 30 minutes. Then, remove the lid and bake for an additional 15-20 minutes until the crust is golden brown.
9. Remove the bread out of your oven let it cool on a wire rack before slicing.

Nutrition Values (per serving): Calories: 230; Proteins: 8g; Carbs: 46g; Fats: 2g; Cholesterol: 0mg; Sodium: 400mg

CHAPTER 7
RUSTIC RECIPES

1. HEARTHSTONE SOURDOUGH LOAF

Prep Time: 40 minutes   **Total Time:** 24 hours   **Serving:** 1 loaf

INGREDIENTS

- 3 and a half cup bread flour
- 1 cup whole wheat flour
- 1.5 cups water (room temperature)
- 1 and a half cup active sourdough starter
- Pinch of salt

DIRECTIONS

1. In a large mixing bowl, combine the bread flour, whole wheat flour, and water. Stir until the mixture forms a shaggy dough. Cover the bowl and let it rest for 30 minutes.
2. Add the active sourdough starter to the bowl and mix it into the dough. Let it rest for 10 minutes.
3. Sprinkle the salt over the dough and knead it for about 10-15 minutes until the dough is elastic and smooth.
4. Place the dough back into the bowl, cover it, and let it rise at room temperature for about 3-4 hours until size has more than doubled.
5. Preheat the oven to 450°F (230°C). Place a baking stone or baking sheet in the oven to preheat as well.
6. Transfer the risen dough onto a floured surface. Shape it into a loaf by folding the edges inward and rolling it tightly.
7. Carefully transfer the shaped loaf onto the preheated baking stone or sheet. Score the top of the loaf with a sharp knife.
8. Bake for 35-40 minutes until the crust is deep golden brown. Remove out of your oven let it cool on a wire rack before slicing.

Nutrition Values (per serving): Calories: 180; Proteins: 6g; Carbs: 38g; Fats: 1g; Cholesterol: 0mg; Sodium: 400mg

2. RUSTIC HARVEST BOULE

Prep Time: 40 minutes   **Total Time:** 24 hours   **Serving:** 1 loaf

INGREDIENTS

- 2 and a half cup bread flour
- 1 cup whole wheat flour
- Half cup rye flour
- 1.5 cups water (room temperature)
- 1.5 cup active sourdough starter
- Pinch of salt
- 1/4 cup mixed seeds (such as pumpkin, sunflower, and flax seeds)

DIRECTIONS

1. In a large mixing bowl, combine the bread flour, whole wheat flour, rye flour, and water. Stir until the mixture forms a shaggy dough. Cover the bowl and let it rest for 30 minutes.
2. Add the active sourdough starter to the bowl and mix it into the dough. Let it rest for 10 minutes.
3. Sprinkle the salt over the dough and knead it for about 10-15 minutes until the dough is elastic and smooth.
4. Add the mixed seeds to the dough and knead for an additional 5 minutes to incorporate them evenly.
5. Place the dough back into the bowl, cover it, and let it rise at room temperature for about 3-4 hours until size has more than doubled.
6. Preheat the oven to 450°F (230°C). Place a Dutch oven or a covered baking dish in the oven to preheat as well.
7. Carefully transfer the risen dough into the preheated Dutch oven. Score the top of the dough with a sharp knife.
8. Cover the Dutch oven and bake for 30 minutes. Then, remove the lid and bake for an additional 15-20 minutes until the crust is golden brown.
9. Remove the bread out of your oven let it cool on a wire rack before slicing.

Nutrition Values (per serving): Calories: 220; Proteins: 7g; Carbs: 43g; Fats: 2g; Cholesterol: 0mg; Sodium: 400mg

3. WOODLAND RUSTIC SOURDOUGH

Prep Time: 30 minutes   **Total Time:** 24 hours   **Serving:** 1 loaf

INGREDIENTS

- 4 cups bread flour
- 1.5 cups water (room temperature)
- 1.5 cups active sourdough starter
- Pinch of salt
- 1/4 cup chopped walnuts
- 1/4 cup dried cranberries

DIRECTIONS

1. Bread flour and water should be mixed together in a big bowl. Stir until the mixture forms a shaggy dough. Cover the bowl and let it rest for 30 minutes.
2. Add the active sourdough starter to the bowl and mix it into the dough. Let it rest for 10 minutes.
3. Sprinkle the salt over the dough and knead it for about 10-15 minutes until the dough is elastic and smooth.
4. Add the chopped walnuts and dried cranberries to the dough and knead for an additional 5 minutes to incorporate them evenly.
5. Place the dough back into the bowl, cover it, and let it rise at room temperature for about 3-4 hours until size has more than doubled.
6. Preheat the oven to 450°F (230°C). Place a Dutch oven or a covered baking dish in the oven to preheat as well.
7. Carefully transfer the risen dough into the preheated Dutch oven. Score the top of the dough with a sharp knife.
8. Cover the Dutch oven and bake for 30 minutes. Then, remove the lid and bake for an additional 15-20 minutes until the crust is golden brown.
9. Remove the bread out of your oven let it cool on a wire rack before slicing.

Nutrition Values (per serving): Calories: 210; Proteins: 7g; Carbs: 43g; Fats: 2g; Cholesterol: 0mg; Sodium: 400mg

4. SEEDED RUSTIC MULTIGRAIN BREAD

Prep Time: 40 minutes   **Total Time:** 24 hours   **Serving:** 1 loaf

INGREDIENTS

- 2.5 cups bread flour
- 1 cup whole wheat flour
- 1 cup rye flour
- 1.5 cups water (room temperature)
- 1.5 cup active sourdough starter
- Pinch of salt
- 1/4 cup mixed seeds (such as sesame, poppy, and sunflower seeds)

DIRECTIONS

1. In a large mixing bowl, combine the bread flour, whole wheat flour, rye flour, and water. Stir until the mixture forms a shaggy dough. Cover the bowl and let it rest for 30 minutes.
2. Add the active sourdough starter to the bowl and mix it into the dough. Let it rest for 10 minutes.
3. Sprinkle the salt over the dough and knead it for about 10-15 minutes until the dough is elastic and smooth.
4. Add the mixed seeds to the dough and knead for an additional 5 minutes to incorporate them evenly.
5. Place the dough back into the bowl, cover it, and let it rise at room temperature for about 3-4 hours until size has more than doubled.
6. Preheat the oven to 450°F (230°C). Place a Dutch oven or a covered baking dish in the oven to preheat as well.
7. Carefully transfer the risen dough into the preheated Dutch oven. Score the top of the dough with a sharp knife.
8. Cover the Dutch oven and bake for 30 minutes. Then, remove the lid and bake for an additional 15-20 minutes until the crust is golden brown.
9. Remove the bread out of your oven let it cool on a wire rack before slicing.

Nutrition Values (per serving): Calories: 220; Proteins: 7g; Carbs: 44g; Fats: 2g; Cholesterol: 0mg; Sodium: 400mg

5. FARMSTEAD WHEAT SOURDOUGH LOAF

Prep Time: 35 minutes   **Total Time:** 24 hours   **Serving:** 1 loaf

INGREDIENTS

- 3.5 cups bread flour
- 0.5 cups whole wheat flour
- 1.5 cups water (room temperature)
- 1.5 cups active sourdough starter
- Pinch of salt

DIRECTIONS

1. In a large mixing bowl, combine the bread flour, whole wheat flour, and water. Stir until the mixture forms a shaggy dough. Cover the bowl and let it rest for 30 minutes.
2. Add the active sourdough starter to the bowl and mix it into the dough. Let it rest for 10 minutes.
3. Sprinkle the salt over the dough and knead it for about 10-15 minutes until the dough is elastic and smooth.
4. Place the dough back into the bowl, cover it, and let it rise at room temperature for about 3-4 hours until size has more than doubled.
5. Preheat the oven to 450°F (230°C). Place a baking stone or baking sheet in the oven to preheat as well.
6. Transfer the risen dough onto a floured surface. Shape it into a loaf by folding the edges inward and rolling it tightly.
7. Carefully transfer the shaped loaf onto the preheated baking stone or sheet. Score the top of the loaf with a sharp knife.
8. Bake for 35-40 minutes until the crust is deep golden brown. Remove out of your oven let it cool on a wire rack before slicing.

Nutrition Values (per serving): Calories: 200; Proteins: 6g; Carbs: 42g; Fats: 1g; Cholesterol: 0mg; Sodium: 400mg

6. OLIVE AND ROSEMARY SOURDOUGH BOULE

Prep Time: 40 minutes   **Total Time:** 24 hours   **Serving:** 1 loaf

INGREDIENTS

- 4 cups bread flour
- 1.5 cups water (room temperature)
- 2 cups active sourdough starter
- Pinch of salt
- 1/2 cup pitted olives, chopped
- 2 tablespoons fresh rosemary, chopped

DIRECTIONS

1. Bread flour and water should be mixed together in a big bowl. Stir until the mixture forms a shaggy dough. Cover the bowl and let it rest for 30 minutes.
2. Add the active sourdough starter to the bowl and mix it into the dough. Let it rest for 10 minutes.
3. Sprinkle the salt over the dough and knead it for about 10-15 minutes until the dough is elastic and smooth.
4. Add the chopped olives and rosemary to the dough and knead for an additional 5 minutes to incorporate them evenly.
5. Place the dough back into the bowl, cover it, and let it rise at room temperature for about 3-4 hours until size has more than doubled.
6. Preheat the oven to 450°F (230°C). Place a Dutch oven or a covered baking dish in the oven to preheat as well.
7. Carefully transfer the risen dough into the preheated Dutch oven. Score the top of the dough with a sharp knife.
8. Cover the Dutch oven and bake for 30 minutes. Then, remove the lid and bake for an additional 15-20 minutes until the crust is golden brown.
9. Remove the bread out of your oven let it cool on a wire rack before slicing.

Nutrition Values (per serving): Calories: 230; Proteins: 7g; Carbs: 45g; Fats: 2g; Cholesterol: 0mg; Sodium: 450mg

7. SUN-DRIED TOMATO AND BASIL SOURDOUGH

Prep Time: 40 minutes   **Total Time:** 24 hours   **Serving:** 1 loaf

INGREDIENTS

- 3.5 cups bread flour
- 1 cup whole wheat flour
- 1.5 cups water (room temperature)
- 2 cup active sourdough starter
- Pinch of salt
- 1/2 cup sun-dried tomatoes, chopped
- 2 tablespoons fresh basil, chopped

DIRECTIONS

1. In a large mixing bowl, combine the bread flour, whole wheat flour, and water. Stir until the mixture forms a shaggy dough. Cover the bowl and let it rest for 30 minutes.
2. Add the active sourdough starter to the bowl and mix it into the dough. Let it rest for 10 minutes.
3. Sprinkle the salt over the dough and knead it for about 10-15 minutes until the dough is elastic and smooth.
4. Add the chopped sun-dried tomatoes and basil to the dough and knead for an additional 5 minutes to incorporate them evenly.
5. Place the dough back into the bowl, cover it, and let it rise at room temperature for about 3-4 hours until size has more than doubled.
6. Preheat the oven to 450°F (230°C). Place a Dutch oven or a covered baking dish in the oven to preheat as well.
7. Carefully transfer the risen dough into the preheated Dutch oven. Score the top of the dough with a sharp knife.
8. Cover the Dutch oven and bake for 30 minutes. Then, remove the lid and bake for an additional 15-20 minutes until the crust is golden brown.
9. Remove the bread out of your oven let it cool on a wire rack before slicing.

Nutrition Values (per serving): Calories: 210; Proteins: 7g; Carbs: 44g; Fats: 1g; Cholesterol: 0mg; Sodium: 400mg

8. RUSTIC RYE SOURDOUGH

Prep Time: 40 minutes   **Total Time:** 24 hours   **Serving:** 1 loaf

INGREDIENTS

- 2.5 cup bread flour
- 1.5 cup rye flour
- 1.5 cups water (room temperature)
- 1.5 cup active sourdough starter
- Pinch of salt

DIRECTIONS

1. In a large mixing bowl, combine the bread flour, rye flour, and water. Stir until the mixture forms a shaggy dough. Cover the bowl and let it rest for 30 minutes.
2. Add the active sourdough starter to the bowl and mix it into the dough. Let it rest for 10 minutes.
3. Sprinkle the salt over the dough and knead it for about 10-15 minutes until the dough is elastic and smooth.
4. Place the dough back into the bowl, cover it, and let it rise at room temperature for about 3-4 hours until size has more than doubled.
5. Preheat the oven to 450°F (230°C). Place a baking stone or baking sheet in the oven to preheat as well.
6. Transfer the risen dough onto a floured surface. Shape it into a loaf by folding the edges inward and rolling it tightly.
7. Carefully transfer the shaped loaf onto the preheated baking stone or sheet. Score the top of the loaf with a sharp knife.
8. Bake for 35-40 minutes until the crust is deep golden brown. Remove out of your oven let it cool on a wire rack before slicing.

Nutrition Values (per serving): Calories: 220; Proteins: 7g; Carbs: 45g; Fats: 1g; Cholesterol: 0mg; Sodium: 400mg

9. WALNUT AND CRANBERRY SOURDOUGH LOAF

Prep Time: 45 minutes   **Total Time:** 24 hours   **Serving:** 1 loaf

INGREDIENTS

- 3.5 cup bread flour
- 0.5 cup whole wheat flour
- 1.5 cups water (room temperature)
- 1.5 cup active sourdough starter
- Pinch of salt
- 1/2 cup walnuts, chopped
- 1/2 cup dried cranberries

DIRECTIONS

1. In a large mixing bowl, combine the bread flour, whole wheat flour, and water. Stir until the mixture forms a shaggy dough. Cover the bowl and let it rest for 30 minutes.
2. Add the active sourdough starter to the bowl and mix it into the dough. Let it rest for 10 minutes.
3. Sprinkle the salt over the dough and knead it for about 10-15 minutes until the dough is elastic and smooth.
4. Add the chopped walnuts and dried cranberries to the dough and knead for an additional 5 minutes to incorporate them evenly.
5. Place the dough back into the bowl, cover it, and let it rise at room temperature for about 3-4 hours until size has more than doubled.
6. Preheat the oven to 450°F (230°C). Place a Dutch oven or a covered baking dish in the oven to preheat as well.
7. Carefully transfer the risen dough into the preheated Dutch oven. Score the top of the dough with a sharp knife.
8. Cover the Dutch oven and bake for 30 minutes. Then, remove the lid and bake for an additional 15-20 minutes until the crust is golden brown.
9. Remove the bread out of your oven let it cool on a wire rack before slicing.

Nutrition Values (per serving): Calories: 230; Proteins: 7g; Carbs: 45g; Fats: 2g; Cholesterol: 0mg; Sodium: 400mg

10. OLIVE AND GARLIC SOURDOUGH

Prep Time: 40 minutes   **Total Time:** 24 hours   **Serving:** 1 loaf

INGREDIENTS

- 4 cup bread flour
- 1.5 cups water (room temperature)
- 1.5 cup active sourdough starter
- Pinch of salt
- 1/2 cup pitted olives, chopped
- 4 cloves garlic, minced

DIRECTIONS

1. Bread flour and water should be mixed together in a big bowl. Whisk until the mixture forms rough, uneven dough. Cover the bowl and let it rest for 30 minutes.
2. Add the active sourdough starter to the bowl and mix it into the dough. Let it rest for 10 minutes.
3. Sprinkle the salt over the dough and knead it for about 10-15 minutes until the dough is elastic and smooth.
4. Add the chopped olives and minced garlic to the dough and knead for an additional 5 minutes to incorporate them evenly.
5. Place the dough back into the bowl, cover it, and let it rise at room temperature for about 3-4 hours until size has more than doubled.
6. Preheat the oven to 450°F (230°C). Place a baking stone or baking sheet in the oven to preheat as well.
7. Transfer the risen dough onto a floured surface. Shape it into a loaf by folding the edges inward and rolling it tightly.
8. Carefully transfer the shaped loaf onto the preheated baking stone or sheet. Score the top of the loaf with a sharp knife.
9. Bake for 35-40 minutes until the crust is deep golden brown. Remove out of your oven let it cool on a wire rack before slicing.

Nutrition Values (per serving): Calories: 220; Proteins: 6g; Carbs: 44g; Fats: 1g; Cholesterol: 0mg; Sodium: 400mg

11. SEEDED MULTIGRAIN SOURDOUGH

Prep Time: 45 minutes   **Total Time:** 24 hours   **Serving:** 1 loaf

INGREDIENTS

- 2.5 cup bread flour
- 0.5 cup whole wheat flour
- 0.5 cup rye flour
- 1.5 cups water (room temperature)
- 1.5 cup active sourdough starter
- Pinch of salt
- 1/4 cup sunflower seeds
- 1/4 cup flaxseeds
- 1/4 cup sesame seeds

DIRECTIONS

1. In a large mixing bowl, combine the bread flour, whole wheat flour, rye flour, and water. Stir until the mixture forms a shaggy dough. Cover the bowl and let it rest for 30 minutes.
2. Add the active sourdough starter to the bowl and mix it into the dough. Let it rest for 10 minutes.
3. Sprinkle the salt over the dough and knead it for about 10-15 minutes until the dough is elastic and smooth.
4. Add the sunflower seeds, flaxseeds, and sesame seeds to the dough and knead for an additional 5 minutes to incorporate them evenly.
5. Place the dough back into the bowl, cover it, and let it rise at room temperature for about 3-4 hours until size has more than doubled.
6. Preheat the oven to 450°F (230°C). Place a Dutch oven or a covered baking dish in the oven to preheat as well.
7. Carefully transfer the risen dough into the preheated Dutch oven. Score the top of the dough with a sharp knife.
8. Cover the Dutch oven and bake for 30 minutes. Then, remove the lid and bake for an additional 15-20 minutes until the crust is golden brown.
9. Remove the bread out of your oven let it cool on a wire rack before slicing.

Nutrition Values (per serving): Calories: 220; Proteins: 8g; Carbs: 42g; Fats: 4g; Cholesterol: 0mg; Sodium: 400mg

12. CINNAMON RAISIN SOURDOUGH

Prep Time: 45 minutes   **Total Time:** 24 hours   **Serving:** 1 loaf

INGREDIENTS

- 3.5 cup bread flour
- 0.5 cup whole wheat flour
- 1.5 cups water (room temperature)
- 1.5 cup active sourdough starter
- Pinch of salt
- 1/2 cup raisins
- 2 teaspoons ground cinnamon

DIRECTIONS

1. In a large mixing bowl, combine the bread flour, whole wheat flour, and water. Stir until the mixture forms a shaggy dough. Cover the bowl and let it rest for 30 minutes.
2. Add the active sourdough starter to the bowl and mix it into the dough. Let it rest for 10 minutes.
3. Sprinkle the salt over the dough and knead it for about 10-15 minutes until the dough is elastic and smooth.
4. Add the raisins and ground cinnamon to the dough and knead for an additional 5 minutes to incorporate them evenly.
5. Place the dough back into the bowl, cover it, and let it rise at room temperature for about 3-4 hours until size has more than doubled.
6. Preheat the oven to 450°F (230°C). Place a Dutch oven or a covered baking dish in the oven to preheat as well.
7. Carefully transfer the risen dough into the preheated Dutch oven. Score the top of the dough with a sharp knife.
8. Cover the Dutch oven and bake for 30 minutes. Then, remove the lid and bake for an additional 15-20 minutes until the crust is golden brown.
9. Remove the bread out of your oven let it cool on a wire rack before slicing.

Nutrition Values (per serving): Calories: 210; Proteins: 7g; Carbs: 44g; Fats: 1g; Cholesterol: 0mg; Sodium: 400mg

13. HERB AND CHEESE SOURDOUGH

Prep Time: 40 minutes   **Total Time:** 24 hours   **Serving:** 1 loaf

INGREDIENTS

- 4 cups bread flour
- 1.5 cups water (room temperature)
- 1.5 cup active sourdough starter
- Pinch of salt
- 2 tablespoons mixed fresh herbs (such as rosemary, thyme, and oregano), chopped
- 1/2 cup shredded cheese (such as cheddar or Parmesan)

DIRECTIONS

1. Bread flour and water should be mixed together in a big bowl. Whisk until the mixture forms rough, uneven dough. Cover the bowl and let it rest for 30 minutes.
2. Add the active sourdough starter to the bowl and mix it into the dough. Let it rest for 10 minutes.
3. Sprinkle the salt over the dough and knead it for about 10-15 minutes until the dough is elastic and smooth.
4. Add the chopped fresh herbs and shredded cheese to the dough and knead for an additional 5 minutes to incorporate them evenly.
5. Place the dough back into the bowl, cover it, and let it rise at room temperature for about 3-4 hours until size has more than doubled.
6. Preheat the oven to 450°F (230°C). Place a baking stone or baking sheet in the oven to preheat as well.
7. Transfer the risen dough onto a floured surface. Shape it into a loaf by folding the edges inward and rolling it tightly.
8. Carefully transfer the shaped loaf onto the preheated baking stone or sheet. Score the top of the loaf with a sharp knife.
9. Bake for 35-40 minutes until the crust is deep golden brown. Remove out of your oven let it cool on a wire rack before slicing.

Nutrition Values (per serving): Calories: 230; Proteins: 8g; Carbs: 46g; Fats: 1g; Cholesterol: 5mg; Sodium: 400mg

14. FIG AND WALNUT SOURDOUGH

Prep Time: 45 minutes   **Total Time:** 24 hours   **Serving:** 1 loaf

INGREDIENTS

- 3.5 cup bread flour
- 0.5 cup whole wheat flour
- 1.5 cups water (room temperature)
- 1.5 cup active sourdough starter
- Pinch of salt
- 1/2 cup dried figs, chopped
- 1/2 cup walnuts, chopped

DIRECTIONS

1. In a large mixing bowl, combine the bread flour, whole wheat flour, and water. Stir until the mixture forms a shaggy dough. Cover the bowl and let it rest for 30 minutes.
2. Add the active sourdough starter to the bowl and mix it into the dough. Let it rest for 10 minutes.
3. Sprinkle the salt over the dough and knead it for about 10-15 minutes until the dough is elastic and smooth.
4. Add the chopped dried figs and walnuts to the dough and knead for an additional 5 minutes to incorporate them evenly.
5. Place the dough back into the bowl, cover it, and let it rise at room temperature for about 3-4 hours until size has more than doubled.
6. Preheat the oven to 450°F (230°C). Place a Dutch oven or a covered baking dish in the oven to preheat as well.
7. Carefully transfer the risen dough into the preheated Dutch oven. Score the top of the dough with a sharp knife.
8. Cover the Dutch oven and bake for 30 minutes. Then, remove the lid and bake for an additional 15-20 minutes until the crust is golden brown.
9. Remove the bread out of your oven let it cool on a wire rack before slicing.

Nutrition Values (per serving): Calories: 240; Proteins: 7g; Carbs: 48g; Fats: 2g; Cholesterol: 0mg; Sodium: 400mg

15. SUN-DRIED TOMATO SOURDOUGH

Prep Time: 40 minutes   **Total Time:** 24 hours   **Serving:** 1 loaf

INGREDIENTS

- 4 cups bread flour
- 1.5 cups water (room temperature)
- 1.5 cups active sourdough starter
- Pinch of salt
- 1/2 cup sun-dried tomatoes, chopped

DIRECTIONS

1. Bread flour and water should be mixed together in a big bowl. Whisk until the mixture forms rough, uneven dough. Cover the bowl and let it rest for 30 minutes.
2. Add the active sourdough starter to the bowl and mix it into the dough. Let it rest for 10 minutes.
3. Sprinkle the salt over the dough and knead it for about 10-15 minutes until the dough is elastic and smooth.
4. Add the chopped sun-dried tomatoes to the dough and knead for an additional 5 minutes to incorporate them evenly.
5. Place the dough back into the bowl, cover it, and let it rise at room temperature for about 3-4 hours till it was twice as big.
6. Preheat the oven to 450°F (230°C). Place a baking stone or baking sheet in the oven to preheat as well.
7. Transfer the risen dough onto a floured surface. Shape it into a loaf by folding the edges inward and rolling it tightly.
8. Carefully transfer the shaped loaf onto the preheated baking stone or sheet. Score the top of the loaf with a sharp knife.
9. Bake for 35-40 minutes until the crust is deep golden brown. Remove out of your oven let it cool on a wire rack before slicing.

Nutrition Values (per serving): Calories: 220; Proteins: 8g; Carbs: 44g; Fats: 1g; Cholesterol: 0mg; Sodium: 400mg

16. ROSEMARY AND GARLIC SOURDOUGH

Prep Time: 45 minutes   **Total Time:** 24 hours   **Serving:** 1 loaf

INGREDIENTS

- 3.5 cups bread flour
- 1 cup whole wheat flour
- 1.5 cups water (room temperature)
- 1.5 cups active sourdough starter
- Pinch of salt
- 2 tablespoons fresh rosemary, chopped
- 4 cloves garlic, minced

DIRECTIONS

1. In a large mixing bowl, combine the bread flour, whole wheat flour, and water. Stir until the mixture forms a shaggy dough. Cover the bowl and let it rest for 30 minutes.
2. Add the active sourdough starter to the bowl and mix it into the dough. Let it rest for 10 minutes.
3. Sprinkle the salt over the dough and knead it for about 10-15 minutes until the dough is elastic and smooth.
4. Add the chopped fresh rosemary and minced garlic to the dough and knead for an additional 5 minutes to incorporate them evenly.
5. Place the dough back into the bowl, cover it, and let it rise at room temperature for about 3-4 hours till it was twice as big.
6. Preheat the oven to 450°F (230°C). Place a Dutch oven or a covered baking dish in the oven to preheat as well.
7. Carefully transfer the risen dough into the preheated Dutch oven. Score the top of the dough with a sharp knife.
8. Cover the Dutch oven and bake for 30 minutes. Then, remove the lid and bake for an additional 15-20 minutes until the crust is golden brown.
9. Remove the bread out of your oven let it cool on a wire rack before slicing.

Nutrition Values (per serving): Calories: 230; Proteins: 7g; Carbs: 46g; Fats: 1g; Cholesterol: 0mg; Sodium: 400mg

17. HERB AND CHEESE SOURDOUGH

Prep Time: 40 minutes   **Total Time:** 24 hours   **Serving:** 1 loaf

INGREDIENTS

- 4 cups bread flour
- 1.5 cups water (room temperature)
- 1.5 cups active sourdough starter
- Pinch of salt
- 2 tablespoons mixed fresh herbs (such as rosemary, thyme, and parsley), chopped
- 1 cup shredded cheese (such as cheddar or Gruyere)

DIRECTIONS

1. Bread flour and water should be mixed together in a big bowl. Whisk until the mixture forms rough, uneven dough. Cover the bowl and let it rest for 30 minutes.
2. Add the active sourdough starter to the bowl and mix it into the dough. Let it rest for 10 minutes.
3. Sprinkle the salt over the dough and knead it for about 10-15 minutes until the dough is elastic and smooth.
4. Add the chopped fresh herbs and shredded cheese to the dough and knead for an additional 5 minutes to incorporate them evenly.
5. Place the dough back into the bowl, cover it, and let it rise at room temperature for about 3-4 hours till it was twice as big.
6. Preheat the oven to 450°F (230°C). Place a baking stone or baking sheet in the oven to preheat as well.
7. Transfer the risen dough onto a floured surface. Shape it into a loaf by folding the edges inward and rolling it tightly.
8. Carefully transfer the shaped loaf onto the preheated baking stone or sheet. Score the top of the loaf with a sharp knife.
9. Bake for 35-40 minutes until the crust is deep golden brown. Remove out of your oven let it cool on a wire rack before slicing.

Nutrition Values (per serving): Calories: 240; Proteins: 9g; Carbs: 46g; Fats: 3g; Cholesterol: 10mg; Sodium: 600mg

18. OLIVE AND FETA SOURDOUGH

Prep Time: 40 minutes   **Total Time:** 24 hours   **Serving:** 1 loaf

INGREDIENTS

- 4 cups bread flour
- 1.5 cups water (room temperature)
- 1.5 cups active sourdough starter
- Pinch of salt
- 1/2 cup pitted olives, chopped (such as Kalamata or green olives)
- 1/2 cup crumbled feta cheese

DIRECTIONS

1. Bread flour and water should be mixed together in a big bowl. Whisk until the mixture forms rough, uneven dough. Cover the bowl and let it rest for 30 minutes.
2. Add the active sourdough starter to the bowl and mix it into the dough. Let it rest for 10 minutes.
3. Sprinkle the salt over the dough and knead it for about 10-15 minutes until the dough is elastic and smooth.
4. Add the chopped olives and crumbled feta cheese to the dough and knead for an additional 5 minutes to incorporate them evenly.
5. Place the dough back into the bowl, cover it, and let it rise at room temperature for about 3-4 hours till it was twice as big.
6. Preheat the oven to 450°F (230°C). Place a baking stone or baking sheet in the oven to preheat as well.
7. Transfer the risen dough onto a floured surface. Shape it into a loaf by folding the edges inward and rolling it tightly.
8. Carefully transfer the shaped loaf onto the preheated baking stone or sheet. Score the top of the loaf with a sharp knife.
9. Bake for 35-40 minutes until the crust is deep golden brown. Remove out of your oven let it cool on a wire rack before slicing.

Nutrition Values (per serving): Calories: 240; Proteins: 9g; Carbs: 46g; Fats: 3g; Cholesterol: 10mg; Sodium: 600mg

19. CINNAMON RAISIN SOURDOUGH

Prep Time: 45 minutes   **Total Time:** 24 hours   **Serving:** 1 loaf

INGREDIENTS

- 3.5 cups bread flour
- 1 cup whole wheat flour
- 1.5 cups water (room temperature)
- 1.5 cup active sourdough starter
- Pinch of salt
- 1/2 cup raisins
- 2 tablespoons ground cinnamon
- 2 tablespoons brown sugar

DIRECTIONS

1. In a large mixing bowl, combine the bread flour, whole wheat flour, and water. Stir until the mixture forms a shaggy dough. Cover the bowl and let it rest for 30 minutes.
2. Add the active sourdough starter to the bowl and mix it into the dough. Let it rest for 10 minutes.
3. Sprinkle the salt over the dough and knead it for about 10-15 minutes until the dough is elastic and smooth.
4. Add the raisins, ground cinnamon, and brown sugar to the dough and knead for an additional 5 minutes to incorporate them evenly.
5. Place the dough back into the bowl, cover it, and let it rise at room temperature for about 3-4 hours till it was twice as big.
6. Preheat the oven to 450°F (230°C). Place a Dutch oven or a covered baking dish in the oven to preheat as well.
7. Carefully transfer the risen dough into the preheated Dutch oven. Score the top of the dough with a sharp knife.
8. Cover the Dutch oven and bake for 30 minutes. Then, remove the lid and bake for an additional 15-20 minutes until the crust is golden brown.
9. Remove the bread out of your oven let it cool on a wire rack before slicing.

Nutrition Values (per serving): Calories: 230; Proteins: 7g; Carbs: 46g; Fats: 1g; Cholesterol: 0mg; Sodium: 400mg

Thank you from the bottom of my heart for choosing to read this book!

It is with immense gratitude that I address these words to you. It gives me enormous pleasure to know that you have decided to give your time and attention to these pages that I have written with commitment and dedication.

Creating this book has been an exciting journey, and my hope is that you have found it as enjoyable and inspiring to read as I have in writing it. Every word was carefully chosen with the goal of conveying a message, a story or a new perspective to you.

I am aware that you have a multitude of choices available to you when it comes to books, and the fact that you chose mine is a source of great pride and happiness. Your choice is invaluable to me, as it is the support and interest of readers like you that give meaning to my work as a writer.

If you have enjoyed the journey you have taken with these pages, I kindly ask you to **share your experience with others**. Reader reviews are a vital tool for raising awareness of a book and helping other readers make an informed choice.

If you feel inspired to do so, you might **take a few minutes to write a positive review** in which you could share your opinions. Even a few words can make a huge difference and help introduce the book to a wider audience.

CHAPTER 8
PIZZA DOUGH AND FLATBREADS

1. MEDITERRANEAN DELIGHT

Prep Time: 20 minutes   **Total Time:** 2 hours   **Servings:** 4

INGREDIENTS

- 1 cup sourdough starter
- 2 cups all-purpose flour
- 1/2 teaspoon salt
- 1/2 cup warm water
- 2 tablespoons olive oil
- 1/2 cup cherry tomatoes, halved
- 1/4 cup sliced black olives
- 1/4 cup crumbled feta cheese
- 2 tablespoons chopped fresh basil

DIRECTIONS

1. In a large mixing bowl, combine the sourdough starter, flour, salt, warm water, and olive oil. Mix well until a smooth dough forms.
2. Cover the bowl with a clean kitchen towel and let the dough rise for about 1-2 hours till it was twice as big.
3. Preheat the oven to 450°F (230°C).
4. Punch down the dough and divide it into 4 equal portions. Roll out each portion into a thin round shape.
5. Place the dough rounds on a baking sheet and top with cherry tomatoes, black olives, feta cheese, and fresh basil.
6. Bake in the preheated oven for 12-15 minutes until the crust is golden and crispy.
7. Remove from the oven, let it cool slightly, and serve.

Nutrition Value (per serving): Calories: 320; Proteins: 9g; Carbs: 52g; Fats: 8g; Cholesterol: 8mg; Sodium: 520mg

2. RUSTIC SOURDOUGH MARGHERITA

Prep Time: 30 minutes   **Total Time:** 3 hours   **Servings:** 4

INGREDIENTS

- 1 cup sourdough starter
- 2 1/2 cups bread flour
- 1 teaspoon salt
- 1/2 cup warm water
- 2 tablespoons olive oil
- 2 cloves garlic, minced
- 4 large tomatoes, sliced
- 8 ounces fresh mozzarella cheese, sliced
- Fresh basil leaves, for garnish
- Salt and pepper, to taste

DIRECTIONS

1. In a large mixing bowl, combine the sourdough starter, bread flour, salt, warm water, and olive oil. Mix well until a smooth dough forms.
2. Knead the dough on a floured surface for about 5 minutes until elastic. Place the dough back in the bowl, cover, and let it rise for 2 hours or till it was twice as big.
3. Preheat the oven to 500°F (260°C).
4. Punch down the dough and divide it into 4 portions. Roll out each portion into a rustic oval shape.
5. Place the dough on a baking sheet and brush with minced garlic and olive oil.
6. Arrange tomato slices and mozzarella cheese on top. Season with salt and pepper.
7. Bake in the preheated oven for 12-15 minutes until the crust is golden and the cheese is bubbly.
8. Remove from the oven, garnish with fresh basil leaves, and serve.

Nutrition Value (per serving): Calories: 380; Proteins: 17g; Carbs: 47g; Fats: 14g; Cholesterol: 30mg; Sodium: 490mg

3. TANGY GARLIC HERB SOURDOUGH FLATBREAD

Prep Time: 15 minutes   **Total Time:** 1 hour 30 minutes   **Servings:** 6

INGREDIENTS

- 1 1/2 cups sourdough starter
- 2 cups all-purpose flour
- 1 teaspoon salt
- 2 tablespoons olive oil
- 4 cloves garlic, minced
- 1 tablespoon chopped fresh parsley
- 1 tablespoon chopped fresh thyme
- 1 tablespoon chopped fresh rosemary

DIRECTIONS

1. In a large mixing bowl, combine the sourdough starter, flour, salt, and olive oil. Mix well until a smooth dough forms.
2. Knead the dough on a floured surface for about 5 minutes until elastic. Place the dough back in the bowl, cover, and let it rise for 1 hour till it was twice as big.
3. Preheat the oven to 450°F (230°C).
4. Punch down the dough and divide it into 6 portions. Roll out each portion into a thin flatbread shape.
5. Place the dough on a baking sheet and brush with minced garlic, chopped parsley, thyme, and rosemary.
6. Bake in the preheated oven for 10-12 minutes until the flatbread is golden and crispy.
7. Remove from the oven, let it cool slightly, and serve.

Nutrition Value (per serving): Calories: 260; Proteins: 7g; Carbs: 48g; Fats: 4g; Cholesterol: 0mg; Sodium: 390mg

4. SMOKY BBQ SOURDOUGH PIZZA

Prep Time: 30 minutes   **Total Time:** 3 hours   **Servings:** 4

INGREDIENTS

- 1 cup sourdough starter
- 2 1/2 cups bread flour
- 1 teaspoon salt
- 1/2 cup warm water
- 2 tablespoons olive oil
- 1/2 cup smoky BBQ sauce
- 1 cup shredded smoked Gouda cheese
- 1/2 cup sliced red onion
- 1/2 cup sliced bell peppers
- 1/2 cup cooked and shredded chicken
- Fresh cilantro, for garnish

DIRECTIONS

1. In a large mixing bowl, combine the sourdough starter, bread flour, salt, warm water, and olive oil. Mix well until a smooth dough forms.
2. Knead the dough on a floured surface for about 5 minutes until elastic. Place the dough back in the bowl, cover, and let it rise for 2 hours or till it was twice as big.
3. Preheat the oven to 500°F (260°C).
4. Punch down the dough and divide it into 4 portions. Roll out each portion into a round pizza shape.
5. Place the dough on a baking sheet or pizza stone. Spread BBQ sauce evenly over the dough.
6. Sprinkle shredded smoked Gouda cheese over the sauce, and top with sliced red onion, bell peppers, and shredded chicken.
7. Bake in the preheated oven for 12-15 minutes until the crust is golden and the cheese is melted and bubbly.
8. Remove from the oven, garnish with fresh cilantro, and serve.

Nutrition Value (per serving): Calories: 420; Proteins: 20g; Carbs: 50g; Fats: 16g; Cholesterol: 50mg; Sodium: 720mg

5. CHEESY SPINACH AND ARTICHOKE SOURDOUGH NAAN

Prep Time: 25 minutes   **Total Time:** 2 hours 30 minutes   **Servings:** 4

INGREDIENTS

- 1 cup sourdough starter
- 2 cups all-purpose flour
- 1 teaspoon salt
- 1/2 cup warm water
- 2 tablespoons olive oil
- 1 cup shredded mozzarella cheese
- 1 cup chopped spinach
- 1/2 cup chopped artichoke hearts
- 2 cloves garlic, minced
- Salt and pepper, to taste

DIRECTIONS

1. In a large mixing bowl, combine the sourdough starter, flour, salt, warm water, and olive oil. Mix well until a smooth dough forms.
2. Knead the dough on a floured surface for about 5 minutes until elastic. Place the dough back in the bowl, cover, and let it rise for 2 hours or until size has more than doubled.
3. Preheat the oven to 450°F (230°C).
4. Punch down the dough and divide it into 4 portions. Roll out each portion into a naan bread shape.
5. Place the dough on a baking sheet and sprinkle shredded mozzarella cheese evenly over each naan.
6. Top with chopped spinach, chopped artichoke hearts, minced garlic, salt, and pepper.
7. Bake in the preheated oven for 12-15 minutes until the naan is golden and the cheese is melted.
8. Remove from the oven, let it cool slightly, and serve.

Nutrition Value (per serving): Calories: 320; Proteins: 12g; Carbs: 40g; Fats: 12g; Cholesterol: 15mg; Sodium: 660mg

6. ZESTY SOURDOUGH PESTO FLATBREAD

Prep Time: 20 minutes   **Total Time:** 2 hours 30 minutes   **Servings:** 4

INGREDIENTS

- 1 cup sourdough starter
- 2 cups all-purpose flour
- 1 teaspoon salt
- 1/2 cup warm water
- 2 tablespoons olive oil
- 1/2 cup basil pesto
- 1 cup shredded mozzarella cheese
- 1/2 cup sliced cherry tomatoes
- 1/4 cup sliced black olives
- Fresh basil leaves, for garnish

DIRECTIONS

1. In a large mixing bowl, combine the sourdough starter, flour, salt, warm water, and olive oil. Mix well until a smooth dough forms.
2. Knead the dough on a floured surface for about 5 minutes until elastic. Place the dough back in the bowl, cover, and let it rise for 2 hours or until size has more than doubled.
3. Preheat the oven to 450°F (230°C).
4. Punch down the dough and divide it into 4 portions. Roll out each portion into a flatbread shape.
5. Place the dough on a baking sheet and spread basil pesto evenly over each flatbread.
6. Sprinkle shredded mozzarella cheese, sliced cherry tomatoes, and sliced black olives on top.
7. Bake in the preheated oven for 12-15 minutes until the flatbread is golden and the cheese is melted and bubbly.
8. Remove from the oven, garnish with fresh basil leaves, and serve.

Nutrition Value (per serving): Calories: 380; Proteins: 16g; Carbs: 42g; Fats: 18g; Cholesterol: 25mg; Sodium: 780mg

7. TACO FIESTA FLATBREAD

Prep Time: 25 minutes   **Total Time:** 3 hours   **Servings:** 4

INGREDIENTS

- 1 cup sourdough starter
- 2 1/2 cups bread flour
- 1 teaspoon salt
- 1/2 cup warm water
- 2 tablespoons olive oil
- 1/2 cup refried beans
- 1/2 cup cooked ground beef or shredded chicken
- 1/4 cup diced tomatoes
- 1/4 cup diced red onion
- 1/4 cup sliced black olives
- 1/4 cup diced bell peppers
- 1/2 cup shredded cheddar cheese
- 1/4 cup chopped fresh cilantro
- 1/4 cup sour cream (optional)

DIRECTIONS

1. In a large mixing bowl, combine the sourdough starter, bread flour, salt, warm water, and olive oil. Mix well until a smooth dough forms.
2. Knead the dough on a floured surface for about 5 minutes until elastic. Place the dough back in the bowl, cover, and let it rise for 2 hours or until size has more than doubled.
3. Preheat the oven to 500°F (260°C).
4. Punch down the dough and divide it into 4 portions. Roll out each portion into a flatbread shape.
5. Place the dough on a baking sheet. Spread a layer of refried beans over each flatbread.
6. Top with cooked ground beef or shredded chicken, diced tomatoes, red onion, black olives, bell peppers, and shredded cheddar cheese.
7. Bake in the preheated oven for 12-15 minutes until the flatbread is golden and the cheese is melted and bubbly.
8. Remove from the oven, garnish with chopped cilantro, and serve with a dollop of sour cream if desired.

Nutrition Value (per serving): Calories: 420; Proteins: 20g; Carbs: 50g; Fats: 16g; Cholesterol: 50mg; Sodium: 880mg

8. SAVORY SOURDOUGH MUSHROOM AND TRUFFLE PIZZA

Prep Time: 30 minutes   **Total Time:** 3 hours   **Servings:** 4

INGREDIENTS

- 1 cup sourdough starter
- 2 1/2 cups bread flour
- 1 teaspoon salt
- 1/2 cup warm water
- 2 tablespoons olive oil
- 1 cup sliced mushrooms (such as cremini or shiitake)
- 2 cloves garlic, minced
- 2 tablespoons truffle oil
- 1 cup shredded mozzarella cheese
- 1/4 cup grated Parmesan cheese
- Fresh parsley, for garnish

DIRECTIONS

1. In a large mixing bowl, combine the sourdough starter, bread flour, salt, warm water, and olive oil. Mix well until a smooth dough forms.
2. Knead the dough on a floured surface for about 5 minutes until elastic. Place the dough back in the bowl, cover, and let it rise for 2 hours or until size has more than doubled.
3. Preheat the oven to 500°F (260°C).
4. Heat a skillet with moderate heat and sauté the sliced mushrooms and minced garlic in truffle oil until tender. Remove from heat and set aside.
5. Punch down the dough and divide it into 4 portions. Roll out each portion into a round pizza shape.
6. Place the dough on a baking sheet or pizza stone. Spread a thin layer of truffle oil over the dough.
7. Sprinkle shredded mozzarella cheese over the oil, and top with the sautéed mushrooms and garlic. Sprinkle grated Parmesan cheese on top.
8. Bake in the preheated oven for 12-15 minutes until the crust is golden and the cheese is melted and bubbly.
9. Remove from the oven, garnish with fresh parsley, and serve.

Nutrition Value (per serving): Calories: 380; Proteins: 16g; Carbs: 42g; Fats: 16g; Cholesterol: 15mg; Sodium: 650mg

9. GREEK GYRO FLATBREAD

Prep Time: 25 minutes   **Total Time:** 3 hours   **Servings:** 4

INGREDIENTS

- 1 cup sourdough starter
- 2 1/2 cups bread flour
- 1 teaspoon salt
- 1/2 cup warm water
- 2 tablespoons olive oil
- 1/2 cup tzatziki sauce
- 1 cup sliced cooked gyro meat or grilled chicken
- 1/4 cup sliced red onion
- 1/4 cup sliced cucumbers
- 1/4 cup sliced tomatoes
- 1/4 cup crumbled feta cheese
- Fresh dill, for garnish

DIRECTIONS

1. In a large mixing bowl, combine the sourdough starter, bread flour, salt, warm water, and olive oil. Mix well until a smooth dough forms.
2. Knead the dough on a floured surface for about 5 minutes until elastic. Place the dough back in the bowl, cover, and let it rise for 2 hours or until size has more than doubled.
3. Preheat the oven to 500°F (260°C).
4. Punch down the dough and divide it into 4 portions. Roll out each portion into a flatbread shape.
5. Place the dough on a baking sheet. Spread a layer of tzatziki sauce over each flatbread.
6. Top with sliced gyro meat or grilled chicken, red onion, cucumbers, tomatoes, and crumbled feta cheese.
7. Bake in the preheated oven for 12-15 minutes until the flatbread is golden.
8. Remove from the oven, garnish with fresh dill, and serve.

Nutrition Value (per serving): Calories: 420; Proteins: 18g; Carbs: 50g; Fats: 16g; Cholesterol: 40mg; Sodium: 750mg

10. SPICY SOURDOUGH PEPPERONI CRUNCH

Prep Time: 30 minutes   **Total Time:** 4 hours   **Servings:** 4

INGREDIENTS

- 1 cup sourdough starter
- 2 1/2 cups bread flour
- 1 teaspoon salt
- 1/2 cup warm water
- 2 tablespoons olive oil
- 1/2 cup marinara sauce
- 1 cup shredded mozzarella cheese
- 1/2 cup sliced pepperoni
- 1/4 cup sliced jalapeños
- 1/4 cup sliced black olives
- 1/4 cup crushed potato chips
- Fresh basil, for garnish

DIRECTIONS

1. In a large mixing bowl, combine the sourdough starter, bread flour, salt, warm water, and olive oil. Mix well until a smooth dough forms.
2. Knead the dough on a floured surface for about 5 minutes until elastic. Place the dough back in the bowl, cover, and let it rise for 3 hours or until size has more than doubled.
3. Preheat the oven to 500°F (260°C).
4. Punch down the dough and divide it into 4 portions. Roll out each portion into a round pizza shape.
5. Place the dough on a baking sheet or pizza stone. Spread marinara sauce evenly over the dough.
6. Sprinkle shredded mozzarella cheese over the sauce, and top with sliced pepperoni, jalapeños, black olives, and crushed potato chips.
7. Bake in the preheated oven for 12-15 minutes until the crust is golden and the cheese is melted and bubbly.
8. Remove from the oven, garnish with fresh basil, and serve.

Nutrition Value (per serving): Calories: 410; Proteins: 18g; Carbs: 48g; Fats: 16g; Cholesterol: 30mg; Sodium: 840mg

11. CAPRESE FOCACCIA

Prep Time: 30 minutes   **Total Time:** 4 hours   **Servings:** 6

INGREDIENTS

- 1 cup sourdough starter
- 3 cups bread flour
- 1 teaspoon salt
- 1/2 cup warm water
- 2 tablespoons olive oil
- 1 cup cherry tomatoes, halved
- 1 cup fresh mozzarella balls, halved
- 1/4 cup sliced fresh basil
- 2 tablespoons balsamic glaze
- Salt and pepper, to taste

DIRECTIONS

1. In a large mixing bowl, combine the sourdough starter, bread flour, salt, warm water, and olive oil. Mix well until a smooth dough forms.
2. Knead the dough on a floured surface for about 5 minutes until elastic. Place the dough back in the bowl, cover, and let it rise for 3 hours or until size has more than doubled.
3. Preheat the oven to 425°F (220°C).
4. Punch down the dough and transfer it to a greased baking sheet. Press the dough out to form a rectangular shape.
5. Top the dough with cherry tomatoes, fresh mozzarella, and sliced basil. Drizzle balsamic glaze over the top.
6. Season with salt and pepper to taste.
7. Bake in the preheated oven for 20-25 minutes until the focaccia is golden and the cheese is melted.
8. Remove from the oven, let it cool slightly, and serve.

Nutrition Value (per serving): Calories: 320; Proteins: 10g; Carbs: 50g; Fats: 8g; Cholesterol: 15mg; Sodium: 520mg

12. VEGGIE SUPREME FLATBREAD

Prep Time: 30 minutes   **Total Time:** 3 hours 30 minutes   **Servings:** 4

INGREDIENTS

- 1 cup sourdough starter
- 2 1/2 cups bread flour
- 1 teaspoon salt
- 1/2 cup warm water
- 2 tablespoons olive oil
- 1/2 cup marinara sauce
- 1 cup shredded mozzarella cheese
- 1/4 cup sliced red bell peppers
- 1/4 cup sliced green bell peppers
- 1/4 cup sliced red onion
- 1/4 cup sliced black olives
- 1/4 cup sliced mushrooms
- Fresh basil, for garnish

DIRECTIONS

1. In a large mixing bowl, combine the sourdough starter, bread flour, salt, warm water, and olive oil. Mix well until a smooth dough forms.
2. Knead the dough on a floured surface for about 5 minutes until elastic. Place the dough back in the bowl, cover, and let it rise for 2 hours or until size has more than doubled.
3. Preheat the oven to 500°F (260°C).
4. Punch down the dough and divide it into 4 portions. Roll out each portion into a flatbread shape.
5. Place the dough on a baking sheet. Spread marinara sauce evenly over the dough.
6. Sprinkle shredded mozzarella cheese over the sauce, and top with sliced bell peppers, red onion, black olives, and mushrooms.
7. Bake in the preheated oven for 12-15 minutes until the flatbread is golden and the cheese is melted and bubbly.
8. Remove from the oven, garnish with fresh basil, and serve.

Nutrition Value (per serving): Calories: 380; Proteins: 16g; Carbs: 50g; Fats: 12g; Cholesterol: 15mg; Sodium: 750mg

13. TANGY SOURDOUGH BBQ CHICKEN NAAN

| Prep Time: 40 minutes | Total Time: 4 hours | Servings: 4 |

INGREDIENTS

- 1 cup sourdough starter
- 2 1/2 cups bread flour
- 1 teaspoon salt
- 1/2 cup warm water
- 2 tablespoons olive oil
- 1/2 cup barbecue sauce
- 1 cup cooked shredded chicken
- 1/4 cup diced red onion
- 1/4 cup diced bell peppers
- 1/4 cup corn kernels
- 1 cup shredded mozzarella cheese
- Fresh cilantro, for garnish

DIRECTIONS

1. In a large mixing bowl, combine the sourdough starter, bread flour, salt, warm water, and olive oil. Mix well until a smooth dough forms.
2. Knead the dough on a floured surface for about 5 minutes until elastic. Place the dough back in the bowl, cover, and let it rise for 3 hours or until size has more than doubled.
3. Preheat the oven to 500°F (260°C).
4. Punch down the dough and divide it into 4 portions. Roll out each portion into a naan shape.
5. Place the dough on a baking sheet. Spread barbecue sauce evenly over each naan.
6. Top with shredded chicken, diced red onion, bell peppers, corn kernels, and shredded mozzarella cheese.
7. Bake in the preheated oven for 12-15 minutes until the naan is golden and the cheese is melted and bubbly.
8. Remove from the oven, garnish with fresh cilantro, and serve.

Nutrition Value (per serving): Calories: 440; Proteins: 22g; Carbs: 52g; Fats: 16g; Cholesterol: 55mg; Sodium: 910mg

14. HAWAIIAN LUAU PIZZA

| Prep Time: 30 minutes | Total Time: 3 hours 30 minutes | Servings: 4 |

INGREDIENTS

- 1 cup sourdough starter
- 2 1/2 cups bread flour
- 1 teaspoon salt
- 1/2 cup warm water
- 2 tablespoons olive oil
- 1/2 cup marinara sauce
- 1 cup shredded mozzarella cheese
- 1/2 cup diced ham.
- 1/2 cup diced pineapple.
- 1/4 cup sliced red onion.
- 1/4 cup sliced black olives.
- Fresh cilantro, for garnish

DIRECTIONS

1. In a large mixing bowl, combine the sourdough starter, bread flour, salt, warm water, and olive oil. Mix well until a smooth dough forms.
2. Knead the dough on a floured surface for about 5 minutes until elastic. Place the dough back in the bowl, cover, and let it rise for 2 hours or until size has more than doubled.
3. Preheat the oven to 500°F (260°C).
4. Punch down the dough and divide it into 4 portions. Roll out each portion into a round pizza shape.
5. Place the dough on a baking sheet or pizza stone. Spread marinara sauce evenly over the dough.
6. Sprinkle shredded mozzarella cheese over the sauce, and top with diced ham, diced pineapple, sliced red onion, and black olives.
7. Bake in the preheated oven for 12-15 minutes until the crust is golden and the cheese is melted and bubbly.
8. Remove from the oven, garnish with fresh cilantro, and serve.

Nutrition Value (per serving): Calories: 410; Proteins: 18g; Carbs: 52g; Fats: 12g; Cholesterol: 25mg; Sodium: 780mg

15. HERBIVORE SOURDOUGH VEGETABLE FLATBREAD

Prep Time: 40 minutes **Total Time:** 4 hours **Servings:** 4

INGREDIENTS

- 1 cup sourdough starter
- 2 1/2 cups bread flour
- 1 teaspoon salt
- 1/2 cup warm water
- 2 tablespoons olive oil
- 1/2 cup marinara sauce
- 1 cup shredded mozzarella cheese
- 1/4 cup sliced bell peppers (red, green, and yellow)
- 1/4 cup sliced zucchini
- 1/4 cup sliced mushrooms
- 1/4 cup sliced red onion
- 1/4 cup sliced black olives
- 1/2 teaspoon dried oregano
- Fresh basil, for garnish

DIRECTIONS

1. In a large mixing bowl, combine the sourdough starter, bread flour, salt, warm water, and olive oil. Mix well until a smooth dough forms.
2. Knead the dough on a floured surface for about 5 minutes until elastic. Place the dough back in the bowl, cover, and let it rise for 3 hours or until size has more than doubled.
3. Preheat the oven to 500°F (260°C).
4. Punch down the dough and divide it into 4 portions. Roll out each portion into a flatbread shape.
5. Place the dough on a baking sheet. Spread marinara sauce evenly over the dough.
6. Sprinkle shredded mozzarella cheese over the sauce, and top with sliced bell peppers, zucchini, mushrooms, red onion, and black olives.
7. Sprinkle dried oregano over the toppings.
8. Bake in the preheated oven for 12-15 minutes until the flatbread is golden and the cheese is melted and bubbly.
9. Remove from the oven, garnish with fresh basil, and serve.

Nutrition Value (per serving): Calories: 380; Proteins: 16g; Carbs: 48g; Fats: 12g; Cholesterol: 15mg; Sodium: 790mg

16. MARGHERITA FOCACCIA

Prep Time: 30 minutes **Total Time:** 4 hours **Servings:** 6

INGREDIENTS

- 1 cup sourdough starter
- 3 cups bread flour
- 1 teaspoon salt
- 1/2 cup warm water
- 2 tablespoons olive oil
- 1/2 cup marinara sauce
- 1 cup cherry tomatoes, halved
- 1 cup fresh mozzarella, sliced
- Fresh basil leaves
- Salt and pepper, to taste

DIRECTIONS

1. In a large mixing bowl, combine the sourdough starter, bread flour, salt, warm water, and olive oil. Mix well until a smooth dough forms.
2. Knead the dough on a floured surface for about 5 minutes until elastic. Place the dough back in the bowl, cover, and let it rise for 3 hours or until size has more than doubled.
3. Preheat the oven to 425°F (220°C).
4. Punch down the dough and transfer it to a greased baking sheet. Press the dough out to form a rectangular shape.
5. Spread marinara sauce evenly over the dough.
6. Arrange the halved cherry tomatoes and sliced mozzarella on top of the sauce.
7. Season with salt and pepper to taste.
8. Bake in the preheated oven for 20-25 minutes until the focaccia is golden and the cheese is melted.
9. Remove from the oven, garnish with fresh basil leaves, and serve.

Nutrition Value (per serving): Calories: 310; Proteins: 13g; Carbs: 46g; Fats: 8g; Cholesterol: 15mg; Sodium: 540mg

17. BUFFALO CHICKEN CRUNCH

Prep Time: 40 minutes   **Total Time:** 4 hours   **Servings:** 4

INGREDIENTS

- 1 cup sourdough starter
- 2 1/2 cups bread flour
- 1 teaspoon salt
- 1/2 cup warm water
- 2 tablespoons olive oil
- 1/2 cup buffalo sauce
- 1 cup cooked shredded chicken
- 1/4 cup diced celery
- 1/4 cup crumbled blue cheese
- 1/4 cup shredded cheddar cheese
- 2 tablespoons chopped green onions
- Ranch dressing, for serving

DIRECTIONS

1. In a large mixing bowl, combine the sourdough starter, bread flour, salt, warm water, and olive oil. Mix well until a smooth dough forms.
2. Knead the dough on a floured surface for about 5 minutes until elastic. Place the dough back in the bowl, cover, and let it rise for 3 hours or until size has more than doubled.
3. Preheat the oven to 500°F (260°C).
4. Punch down the dough and divide it into 4 portions. Roll out each portion into a round pizza shape.
5. Place the dough on a baking sheet or pizza stone. Spread buffalo sauce evenly over the dough.
6. Top with shredded chicken, diced celery, crumbled blue cheese, shredded cheddar cheese, and chopped green onions.
7. Bake in the preheated oven for 12-15 minutes until the crust is golden and the cheese is melted and bubbly.
8. Remove from the oven, drizzle with ranch dressing, and serve.

Nutrition Value (per serving): Calories: 380; Proteins: 19g; Carbs: 50g; Fats: 12g; Cholesterol: 40mg; Sodium: 1280mg

18. FIG AND PROSCIUTTO FLATBREAD

Prep Time: 40 minutes   **Total Time:** 4 hours 30 minutes   **Servings:** 4

INGREDIENTS

- 1 cup sourdough starter
- 2 1/2 cups bread flour
- 1 teaspoon salt
- 1/2 cup warm water
- 2 tablespoons olive oil
- 1/2 cup fig jam
- 4-6 slices prosciutto
- 1/2 cup crumbled goat cheese
- Fresh arugula, for garnish
- Balsamic glaze, for drizzling

DIRECTIONS

1. In a large mixing bowl, combine the sourdough starter, bread flour, salt, warm water, and olive oil. Mix well until a smooth dough forms.
2. Knead the dough on a floured surface for about 5 minutes until elastic. Place the dough back in the bowl, cover, and let it rise for 3 hours or until size has more than doubled.
3. Preheat the oven to 500°F (260°C).
4. Punch down the dough and divide it into 4 portions. Roll out each portion into a flatbread shape.
5. Place the dough on a baking sheet. Spread fig jam evenly over the dough.
6. Tear the prosciutto slices into smaller pieces and distribute them over the jam.
7. Sprinkle crumbled goat cheese on top.
8. Bake in the preheated oven for 12-15 minutes until the flatbread is golden and the cheese is melted.
9. Remove from the oven, garnish with fresh arugula, drizzle with balsamic glaze, and serve.

Nutrition Value (per serving): Calories: 420; Proteins: 17g; Carbs: 52g; Fats: 16g; Cholesterol: 35mg; Sodium: 850mg

19. MEDITERRANEAN VEGGIE NAAN

Prep Time: 30 minutes   **Total Time:** 4 hours 30 minutes   **Servings:** 4

INGREDIENTS

- 1 cup sourdough starter
- 2 1/2 cups bread flour
- 1 teaspoon salt
- 1/2 cup warm water
- 2 tablespoons olive oil
- 1/4 cup hummus
- 1/4 cup red bell pepper slices
- 1/4 cup yellow bell pepper sliced
- 1/4 cup sliced red onion
- 1/4 cup sliced kalamata olives
- 1/4 cup crumbled feta cheese
- Fresh parsley, for garnish

DIRECTIONS

1. In a large mixing bowl, combine the sourdough starter, bread flour, salt, warm water, and olive oil. Mix well until a smooth dough forms.
2. Knead the dough on a floured surface for about 5 minutes until elastic. Place the dough back in the bowl, cover, and let it rise for 4 hours or until size has more than doubled.
3. Preheat the oven to 500°F (260°C).
4. Punch down the dough and divide it into 4 portions. Roll out each portion into a naan shape.
5. Place the dough on a baking sheet. Spread hummus evenly over the dough.
6. Top with sliced red bell pepper, yellow bell pepper, red onion, kalamata olives, and crumbled feta cheese.
7. Bake in the preheated oven for 12-15 minutes until the naan is golden and slightly crispy.
8. Remove from the oven, garnish with fresh parsley, and serve.

Nutrition Value (per serving): Calories: 360; Proteins: 12g; Carbs: 52g; Fats: 10g; Cholesterol: 10mg; Sodium: 810mg

20. SPINACH AND FETA FLATBREAD

Prep Time: 30 minutes   **Total Time:** 4 hours 30 minutes   **Servings:** 4

INGREDIENTS

- 1 cup sourdough starter
- 2 1/2 cups bread flour
- 1 teaspoon salt
- 1/2 cup warm water
- 2 tablespoons olive oil
- 1 cup fresh spinach, chopped
- 1/2 cup crumbled feta cheese
- 1/4 cup sliced black olives
- 2 tablespoons chopped fresh dill
- Lemon wedges, for serving

DIRECTIONS

1. In a large mixing bowl, combine the sourdough starter, bread flour, salt, warm water, and olive oil. Mix well until a smooth dough forms.
2. Knead the dough on a floured surface for about 5 minutes until elastic. Place the dough back in the bowl, cover, and let it rise for 4 hours or until size has more than doubled.
3. Preheat the oven to 500°F (260°C).
4. Punch down the dough and divide it into 4 portions. Roll out each portion into a flatbread shape.
5. Place the dough on a baking sheet. Sprinkle chopped spinach evenly over the dough.
6. Crumble feta cheese on top, and sprinkle sliced black olives and chopped fresh dill over the cheese.
7. Bake in the preheated oven for 12-15 minutes until the flatbread is golden and the cheese is melted.
8. Remove from the oven, squeeze lemon juice over the flatbread, and serve.

Nutrition Value (per serving): Calories: 320; Proteins: 12g; Carbs: 47g; Fats: 9g; Cholesterol: 25mg; Sodium: 710mg

21. BBQ CHICKEN AND PINEAPPLE PIZZA

Prep Time: 40 minutes　　　**Total Time:** 4 hours　　　**Servings:** 4

INGREDIENTS

- 1 cup sourdough starter
- 2 1/2 cups bread flour
- 1 teaspoon salt
- 1/2 cup warm water
- 2 tablespoons olive oil
- 1/2 cup barbecue sauce
- 1 cup cooked shredded chicken
- 1 cup pineapple chunks
- 1/4 cup sliced red onion
- 1 cup shredded mozzarella cheese
- Fresh cilantro, for garnish

DIRECTIONS

1. In a large mixing bowl, combine the sourdough starter, bread flour, salt, warm water, and olive oil. Mix well until a smooth dough forms.
2. Knead the dough on a floured surface for about 5 minutes until elastic. Place the dough back in the bowl, cover, and let it rise for 3 hours or until size has more than doubled.
3. Preheat the oven to 500°F (260°C).
4. Punch down the dough and divide it into 4 portions. Roll out each portion into a round pizza shape.
5. Place the dough on a baking sheet or pizza stone. Spread barbecue sauce evenly over the dough.
6. Top with shredded chicken, pineapple chunks, sliced red onion, and shredded mozzarella cheese.
7. Bake in the preheated oven for 12-15 minutes until the crust is golden and the cheese is melted and bubbly.
8. Remove from the oven, garnish with fresh cilantro, and serve.

Nutrition Value (per serving): Calories: 440; Proteins: 23g; Carbs: 52g; Fats: 15g; Cholesterol: 55mg; Sodium: 1050mg

22. TOMATO AND BASIL FOCACCIA

Prep Time: 40 minutes　　　**Total Time:** 4 hours 30 minutes　　　**Servings:** 4

INGREDIENTS

- 1 cup sourdough starter
- 2 1/2 cups bread flour
- 1 teaspoon salt
- 1/2 cup warm water
- 2 tablespoons olive oil
- 2-3 tomatoes, thinly sliced
- 1/4 cup chopped fresh basil
- 2 cloves garlic, minced
- Sea salt, for sprinkling
- Extra virgin olive oil, for drizzling

DIRECTIONS

1. In a large mixing bowl, combine the sourdough starter, bread flour, salt, warm water, and olive oil. Mix well until a smooth dough forms.
2. Knead the dough on a floured surface for about 5 minutes until elastic. Place the dough back in the bowl, cover, and let it rise for 4 hours or until size has more than doubled.
3. Preheat the oven to 425°F (220°C).
4. Punch down the dough and transfer it to a greased baking sheet. Press and stretch the dough to form a rectangular shape.
5. Arrange the tomato slices on top of the dough. Sprinkle chopped fresh basil and minced garlic over the tomatoes.
6. Sprinkle sea salt over the focaccia.
7. Bake in the preheated oven for 20-25 minutes until the focaccia is golden and the tomatoes are slightly roasted.
8. Remove from the oven, drizzle with extra virgin olive oil, and serve.

Nutrition Value (per serving): Calories: 380; Proteins: 12g; Carbs: 65g; Fats: 7g; Cholesterol: 0mg; Sodium: 600mg

23. MUSHROOM AND GRUYERE FLATBREAD

Prep Time: 30 minutes   **Total Time:** 4 hours 30 minutes   **Servings:** 4

INGREDIENTS

- 1 cup sourdough starter
- 2 1/2 cups bread flour
- 1 teaspoon salt
- 1/2 cup warm water
- 2 tablespoons olive oil
- 1 cup sliced mushrooms
- 1 cup shredded Gruyere cheese
- 2 tablespoons chopped fresh thyme
- Salt and pepper, to taste

DIRECTIONS

1. In a large mixing bowl, combine the sourdough starter, bread flour, salt, warm water, and olive oil. Mix well until a smooth dough forms.
2. Knead the dough on a floured surface for about 5 minutes until elastic. Place the dough back in the bowl, cover, and let it rise for 4 hours or until size has more than doubled.
3. Preheat the oven to 500°F (260°C).
4. Punch down the dough and divide it into 4 portions. Roll out each portion into a flatbread shape.
5. Place the dough on a baking sheet. Sprinkle sliced mushrooms evenly over the dough.
6. Sprinkle shredded Gruyere cheese and chopped fresh thyme over the mushrooms. Season with salt and pepper to taste.
7. Bake in the preheated oven for 12-15 minutes until the flatbread is golden and the cheese is melted.
8. Remove from the oven, slice into pieces, and serve.

Nutrition Value (per serving): Calories: 400; Proteins: 18g; Carbs: 48g; Fats: 14g; Cholesterol: 35mg; Sodium: 700mg

24. MARGHERITA FOCACCIA

Prep Time: 40 minutes   **Total Time:** 4 hours 30 minutes   **Servings:** 4

INGREDIENTS

- 1 cup sourdough starter
- 2 1/2 cups bread flour
- 1 teaspoon salt
- 1/2 cup warm water
- 2 tablespoons olive oil
- 2-3 tomatoes, thinly sliced
- 8-10 fresh basil leaves
- 1 cup shredded mozzarella cheese
- 2 cloves garlic, minced
- Sea salt, for sprinkling
- Extra virgin olive oil, for drizzling

DIRECTIONS

1. In a large mixing bowl, combine the sourdough starter, bread flour, salt, warm water, and olive oil. Mix well until a smooth dough forms.
2. Knead the dough on a floured surface for about 5 minutes until elastic. Place the dough back in the bowl, cover, and let it rise for 4 hours or until size has more than doubled.
3. Preheat the oven to 425°F (220°C).
4. Punch down the dough and transfer it to a greased baking sheet. Press and stretch the dough to form a rectangular shape.
5. Arrange the tomato slices and fresh basil leaves on top of the dough.
6. Sprinkle shredded mozzarella cheese and minced garlic over the tomatoes and basil.
7. Sprinkle sea salt over the focaccia.
8. Bake in the preheated oven for 20-25 minutes until the focaccia is golden and the cheese is melted and bubbly.
9. Remove from the oven, drizzle with extra virgin olive oil, and serve.

Nutrition Value (per serving): Calories: 410; Proteins: 16g; Carbs: 50g; Fats: 16g; Cholesterol: 40mg; Sodium: 780mg

CHAPTER 9
WHOLE GRAIN RECIPES

1. BREAD

Prep Time: 30 minutes	**Total Time:** 24 hours (including resting and fermentation time)	**Serving:** 1 loaf

INGREDIENTS

- 4 cups whole wheat flour
- 1 cup bread flour
- 3 cups water (room temperature)
- 1 cup sourdough starter (active and bubbly)
- Pinch of salt

DIRECTIONS

1. In a large mixing bowl, combine the whole wheat flour, bread flour, and water. Stir until a shaggy dough forms.
2. Cover the bowl with a clean kitchen towel and let it rest for 30 minutes.
3. Add the sourdough starter to the dough and mix well. Cover again and let it rest for another 30 minutes.
4. Sprinkle the salt over the dough and knead it for about 10 minutes until the dough becomes elastic and smooth.
5. Place the dough back into the bowl, cover, and let it ferment at room temperature for 6 to 8 hours, or until it doubles in size.
6. After the first fermentation, shape the dough into a loaf and place it into a greased bread pan.
7. Cover the pan with a kitchen towel and let the dough undergo the second fermentation for 2 to 3 hours, or until it visibly expands.
8. Preheat the oven to 450°F (230°C).
9. Once the dough has sufficiently risen, score the top with a sharp knife or razor blade.
10. Bake for 40 to 45 minutes, or until the crust turns golden brown and sounds hollow when tapped on the bottom.
11. Remove the bread out of your oven let it cool on a wire rack before slicing.

Nutrition Value (Per Serving): Calories: 120; Proteins: 4g; Carbs: 25g; Fats: 1g; Cholesterol: 0mg; Sodium: 200mg

2. BAGELS

Prep Time: 30 minutes   **Total Time:** 24 hours (including resting and fermentation time)   **Serving:** 6 bagels

INGREDIENTS

- 3.5 cups whole wheat flour
- 1 cup bread flour
- 2 cups water (room temperature)
- 1 cup sourdough starter (active and bubbly)
- Pinch of salt
- 1 tablespoon honey or maple syrup (optional)
- Toppings of your choice (e.g., sesame seeds, poppy seeds, dried onion flakes)

DIRECTIONS

1. In a mixing bowl, combine the whole wheat flour, bread flour, water, sourdough starter, salt, and honey/maple syrup (optional). Mix until a dough forms.
2. Transfer the dough to a floured surface and knead for about 10 minutes until it becomes elastic.
3. Place the dough back into the bowl, cover, and let it ferment at room temperature for 6 to 8 hours, or until it doubles in size.
4. Once fermented, divide the dough into 6 equal portions and shape each portion into a ball.
5. To form the bagels, poke a hole in the center of each dough ball with your thumb and gently stretch the hole to make it about 2 inches in diameter. Shape the bagel into a ring.
6. Place the shaped bagels on a baking sheet lined with parchment paper. Cover with a kitchen towel and let them undergo the second fermentation for 2 to 3 hours, or until they visibly expand.
7. Preheat the oven to 425°F (220°C). Carry a large pot of water to a boil.
8. Once the water is boiling, carefully drop the bagels into the water, two or three at a time, and boil them for about 1 minute on each side.
9. Remove the boiled bagels from the water using a slotted spoon and place them back on the baking sheet.
10. Sprinkle your desired toppings onto the bagels.
11. Bake for 20 to 25 minutes, or until the bagels turn golden brown.
12. Allow the bagels to cool on a wire rack before serving.

Nutrition Value (Per Serving - 1 Bagel): Calories: 180; Proteins: 6g; Carbs: 35g; Fats: 1g; Cholesterol: 0mg; Sodium: 250mg

3. PANCAKES

Prep Time: 15 minutes

Total Time: 12 hours (including resting and fermentation time)

Serving: 4 servings (8 pancakes)

INGREDIENTS

- 1 cup whole wheat flour
- 1/4 cup cornmeal
- 1 tablespoon sugar
- 1/2 teaspoon baking soda
- 1/2 teaspoon salt
- 1 cup sourdough starter (active and bubbly)
- 1 cup buttermilk
- 1 large egg
- Butter or oil for cooking

DIRECTIONS

1. In a mixing dish, whisk together the whole wheat flour, cornmeal, sugar, baking soda, and salt.
2. In a separate bowl, whisk the sourdough starter, buttermilk, and egg until well combined.
3. After adding the liquid components, mix the dry ingredients only until they are barely blended. Do not over mix; a few lumps are fine.
4. Cover the bowl with a clean kitchen towel and let the batter rest at room temperature for 8 to 12 hours, or overnight. This allows the sourdough to ferment and develop flavor.
5. Preheat a griddle or large non-stick skillet with moderate heat. Lightly grease with butter or oil.
6. Pour 1/4 cup of the pancake batter onto the heated surface for every pancake. Cook until small bubbles appear on the top, then turn and cook until golden brown on the other side.
7. Repeat with the remaining batter, adding more oil or butter as needed.
8. Serve the pancakes warm with your favorite toppings such as maple syrup, fresh fruits, or yogurt.

Nutrition Value (Per Serving - 2 Pancakes): Calories: 220; Proteins: 7g; Carbs: 40g; Fats: 3g; Cholesterol: 45mg; Sodium: 400mg

4. PIZZA CRUST

Prep Time: 20 minutes

Total Time: 24 hours (including resting and fermentation time)

Serving: 1 pizza crust (12-inch)

INGREDIENTS

- 1 cup whole wheat flour
- 1 cup bread flour
- 1/2 cup sourdough starter (active and bubbly)
- 1 teaspoon salt
- 1 tablespoon olive oil
- 1/2 cup warm water

DIRECTIONS

1. In a large mixing bowl, combine the whole wheat flour, bread flour, sourdough starter, salt, olive oil, and warm water. Mix until the ingredients come together to form a dough.
2. Transfer the dough to a floured surface and knead for about 10 minutes till it becomes smooth and elastic.
3. Place the dough back into the bowl, cover, and let it rest at room temperature for 6 to 8 hours, or until it doubles in size.
4. Once the dough has fermented, punch it down and transfer it to a lightly greased 12-inch pizza pan.
5. Using your hands or a rolling pin, flatten and stretch the dough to fit the pan. Allow the dough to rest for a few minutes if it won't stretch, then try again.
6. Cover the pan with a kitchen towel and let the dough undergo the second fermentation for 2 to 3 hours, or until it visibly expands.
7. Preheat the oven to 475°F (245°C).
8. Once the dough has risen, add your desired pizza toppings.
9. Bake in the preheated oven for 15 to 20 minutes, or until the crust turns golden brown and crispy.
10. Remove from the oven, let it cool for a few minutes, then slice and serve.

Nutrition Value (Per Serving): Calories: 250; Proteins: 8g; Carbs: 45g; Fats: 5g; Cholesterol: 0mg; Sodium: 400mg

5. CRACKERS

Prep Time: 15 minutes

Total Time: 12 hours (including resting and fermentation time)

Serving: Makes about 40 crackers

INGREDIENTS

- 1 cup whole wheat flour
- 1/4 cup bread flour
- 1/4 cup cornmeal
- 1/2 teaspoon salt
- 1/4 cup sourdough starter (active and bubbly)
- 2 tablespoons olive oil
- 1/4 cup water (room temperature)
- Optional toppings: sea salt, sesame seeds, poppy seeds, herbs, etc.

DIRECTIONS

1. In a mixing bowl, combine the whole wheat flour, bread flour, cornmeal, and salt.
2. Add the sourdough starter, olive oil, and water to the dry ingredients. Mix until a dough forms. If the dough is too dry, add a little more water, a tablespoon at a time.
3. Transfer the dough to a floured surface and knead for a few minutes until it becomes smooth.
4. Place the dough back into the bowl, cover, and let it rest at room temperature for 8 to 12 hours, or overnight. This allows the sourdough to ferment and develop flavor.
5. Preheat the oven to 375°F (190°C) and use parchment paper to cover a baking sheet.
6. Roll out the fermented dough thinly on a floured surface or directly on the parchment paper.
7. Using a sharp knife or a pizza cutter, cut the rolled-out dough into small rectangular or square shapes to make crackers.
8. Prick the crackers with a fork to prevent them from puffing up during baking.
9. Sprinkle the optional toppings, such as sea salt, sesame seeds, or herbs, on top of the crackers.
10. Transfer the parchment paper with the crackers onto the baking sheet.
11. Bake for 12 to 15 minutes, or until the crackers turn golden brown and crispy.
12. Remove out of your oven let the crackers cool completely on a wire rack before serving or storing in an airtight container.

Nutrition Value (Per Serving - 4 Crackers): Calories: 100; Proteins: 3g; Carbs: 15g; Fats: 4g; Cholesterol: 0mg; Sodium: 100mg

6. MUFFINS

Prep Time: 20 minutes

Total Time: 12 hours (including resting and fermentation time)

Serving: Makes 12 muffins

INGREDIENTS

- 1 1/2 cups whole wheat flour
- 1/2 cup rolled oats
- 1/2 cup brown sugar or honey
- 1 teaspoon baking powder
- 1/2 teaspoon baking soda
- 1/2 teaspoon salt
- 1 cup sourdough starter (active and bubbly)
- 1/2 cup milk
- 1/4 cup melted butter or vegetable oil
- 1 large egg
- 1 teaspoon vanilla extract
- Optional add-ins: nuts, dried fruits, chocolate chips, etc.

DIRECTIONS

1. In a large mixing bowl, combine wheat flour, rolled oats, brown sugar (or honey), baking powder, baking soda, and salt.
2. In a separate dish, whisk together the sourdough starter, milk, melted butter (or oil), egg, as well as vanilla essence.
3. After adding the liquid components, mix the dry ingredients only until they are barely blended. Be careful not to over mix; a few lumps are fine.
4. If desired, fold in your chosen add-ins, such as nuts, dried fruits, or chocolate chips.
5. Cover the bowl with a clean kitchen towel and let the batter rest at room temperature for 8 to 12 hours, or overnight. This allows the sourdough to ferment and develop flavor.
6. Turn the oven temperature up to 375 degrees Fahrenheit (190 degrees Celsius). Use paper liners or oil a muffin tray.
7. Spoon the batter into the prepared muffin cups, filling each about two-thirds full.
8. Bake for 18 to 20 minutes, or up to the point at which a toothpick inserted into the center of a muffin emerges clean.
9. Remove out of your oven let the muffins cool in the tin for a few minutes before transferring them to a wire rack to cool completely.
10. Serve the muffins warm or at room temperature.

Nutrition Value (Per Serving - 1 Muffin): Calories: 180; Proteins: 4g; Carbs: 28g; Fats: 6g; Cholesterol: 30mg; Sodium: 200mg

7. WAFFLES

Prep Time: 15 minutes

Total Time: 12 hours (including resting and fermentation time)

Serving: Makes 8 waffles

INGREDIENTS

- 1 1/2 cups whole wheat flour
- 1/2 cup rolled oats
- 2 tablespoons sugar
- 1 1/2 teaspoons baking powder
- 1/2 teaspoon baking soda
- 1/2 teaspoon salt
- 1 cup sourdough starter (active and bubbly)
- 1 cup buttermilk
- 2 large eggs
- 1/4 cup melted butter or vegetable oil
- Optional toppings: maple syrup, fresh fruits, yogurt, etc.

DIRECTIONS

1. In a mixing dish, whisk together the whole wheat flour baking soda, salt, baking powder, rolled oats and sugar
2. In a separate dish, whisk together the sourdough starter, buttermilk, eggs, and melted butter (or oil).
3. After adding the liquid components, mix the dry ingredients only until they are barely blended. Be careful not to over mix; a few lumps are fine.
4. Cover the bowl with a clean kitchen towel and let the batter rest at room temperature for 8 to 12 hours, or overnight. This allows the sourdough to ferment and develop flavor.
5. Preheat your waffle iron according to the manufacturer's instructions.
6. Give the batter a quick stir to incorporate any separated liquids.
7. Spoon the batter onto the preheated waffle iron and cook until golden brown and crispy.
8. Remove the cooked waffles from the iron and repeat with the remaining batter.
9. Serve the waffles warm with your favorite toppings, such as maple syrup, fresh fruits, yogurt, or whipped cream.

Nutrition Value (Per Serving - 1 Waffle): Calories: 200; Proteins: 6g; Carbs: 30g; Fats: 7g; Cholesterol: 65mg; Sodium: 350mg

8. CINNAMON ROLLS

Prep Time: 30 minutes   **Total Time:** 12 hours (including resting and fermentation time)   **Serving:** Makes 12 cinnamon rolls

INGREDIENTS

- Dough:
- 2 cups whole wheat flour
- 1 cup bread flour
- 1/4 cup sugar
- 1 teaspoon salt
- 1 cup sourdough starter (active and bubbly)
- 1/2 cup milk
- 1/4 cup melted butter
- 1 large egg
- Filling:
- 1/4 cup melted butter
- 1/2 cup brown sugar
- 1 tablespoon ground cinnamon
- **Glaze:**
- 1 cup powdered sugar
- 1 tablespoon milk
- 1/2 teaspoon vanilla extract

DIRECTIONS

1. In a large mixing bowl, combine the whole wheat flour, bread flour, sugar, and salt.
2. In a separate dish, whisk together the sourdough starter, milk, melted butter, and egg.
3. Pour the wet ingredients into the dry ingredients and stir until a dough forms.
4. Transfer the dough to a floured surface and knead for about 10 minutes till it becomes smooth and elastic.
5. Place the dough back into the bowl, cover, and let it rest at room temperature for 6 to 8 hours, or until it doubles in size.
6. Once the dough has risen, punch it down and roll it out into a rectangular shape.
7. Brush the melted butter evenly over the rolled-out dough.
8. In a small bowl, mix together the brown sugar and ground cinnamon for the filling. Sprinkle the mixture over the buttered dough.
9. Starting from one long edge, tightly roll up the dough into a log.
10. Cut the rolled dough into 12 equal-sized slices.
11. Place the cinnamon rolls in a greased baking dish, leaving a little space between each roll.
12. Cover the dish with a kitchen towel and let the rolls undergo the second fermentation for 2 to 3 hours, or until they visibly expand.
13. Preheat the oven to 375°F (190°C).
14. Bake the cinnamon rolls for 20 to 25 minutes, or until golden brown.
15. While the rolls are baking, prepare the glaze by whisking together the powdered sugar, milk, as well as vanilla essence until smooth.
16. Remove the cinnamon rolls out of your oven let them cool for a few minutes.
17. Drizzle the glaze over the warm rolls and serve.

Nutrition Value (Per Serving - 1 Cinnamon Roll): Calories: 280; Proteins: 5g; Carbs: 48g; Fats: 8g; Cholesterol: 35mg; Sodium: 220mg

9. ENGLISH MUFFINS

Prep Time: 30 minutes

Total Time: 12 hours (including resting and fermentation time)

Serving: Makes about 12 English muffins

INGREDIENTS

- 2 cups whole wheat flour
- 1 cup bread flour
- 1 tablespoon sugar
- 1 teaspoon salt
- 1 cup sourdough starter (active and bubbly)
- 1 cup milk
- 2 tablespoons melted butter
- 1 teaspoon baking soda
- Cornmeal (for dusting)

DIRECTIONS

1. In a large mixing bowl, combine the whole wheat flour, bread flour, sugar, and salt.
2. In a separate dish, whisk together the sourdough starter, milk, and melted butter.
3. Pour the wet ingredients into the dry ingredients and stir until a dough forms.
4. Transfer the dough to a floured surface and knead for about 10 minutes till it becomes smooth and elastic.
5. Place the dough back into the bowl, cover, and let it rest at room temperature for 6 to 8 hours, or until it doubles in size.
6. Once the dough has risen, punch it down and sprinkle the baking soda over the dough. Knead the dough for a few minutes to incorporate the baking soda.
7. Roll out the dough to a thickness of about 1/2 inch (1.3 cm) on a floured surface.
8. Use a round cookie cutter or a glass to cut out circles from the dough. Re-roll and cut the remaining dough scraps.
9. Place the cut-out dough circles on a baking sheet sprinkled with cornmeal.
10. Cover the baking sheet with a kitchen towel and let the muffins undergo the second fermentation for 2 to 3 hours, or until they visibly expand.
11. Preheat a griddle or a large non-stick skillet with moderate heat. Lightly grease with butter or oil.
12. Cook the English muffins on the griddle or skillet for about 5 minutes on each side, or until they turn golden brown and are cooked through.
13. Remove from the griddle or skillet and let the muffins cool on a wire rack.
14. Once cooled, split the English muffins with a fork or a serrated knife and toast before serving.

Nutrition Value (Per Serving - 1 English muffin): Calories: 180; Proteins: 6g; Carbs: 32g; Fats: 3g; Cholesterol: 10mg; Sodium: 300mg

10. BAGUETTES

Prep Time: 30 minutes

Total Time: 24 hours (including resting and fermentation time)

Serving: Makes 2 baguettes

INGREDIENTS

- 2 cups whole wheat flour
- 1 cup bread flour
- 1 teaspoon salt
- 1 cup sourdough starter (active and bubbly)
- 1 cup lukewarm water

DIRECTIONS

1. In a large mixing bowl, combine the whole wheat flour, bread flour, and salt.
2. In a separate dish, whisk together the sourdough starter and lukewarm water.
3. Pour the wet ingredients into the dry ingredients and stir until a dough forms.
4. Transfer the dough to a floured surface and knead for about 10 minutes till it becomes smooth and elastic.
5. Place the dough back into the bowl, cover, and let it rest at room temperature for 12 to 18 hours, or until it doubles in size.
6. Once the dough has risen, punch it down and divide it into two equal portions.
7. Shape each portion into a baguette by elongating the dough and tapering the ends.
8. Place the shaped baguettes onto a baking sheet lined with parchment paper.
9. Cover the baking sheet with a kitchen towel and let the baguettes undergo the second fermentation for 4 to 6 hours, or until they visibly expand.
10. Preheat the oven to 450°F (230°C) and place an empty baking dish on the bottom rack of the oven.
11. Just before baking, score the tops of the baguettes with diagonal slashes using a sharp knife or a bread scoring tool.
12. Transfer the baking sheet with the baguettes to the preheated oven.
13. To generate steam, pour 1 cup of boiling water into the empty baking dish at the bottom of the oven.
14. Bake the baguettes for 25 to 30 minutes, or until they turn golden brown and sound hollow when tapped on the bottom.
15. Remove out of your oven let the baguettes cool on a wire rack before slicing and serving.

Nutrition Value (Per Serving - 1/2 Baguette): Calories: 200; Proteins: 6g; Carbs: 42g; Fats: 1g; Cholesterol: 0mg; Sodium: 300mg

11. CHEESY PIZZA CRUST

Prep Time: 20 minutes   **Total Time:** 24 hours (including resting and fermentation time)   **Serving:** Makes 2 medium-sized pizza crusts

INGREDIENTS

- 2 cups whole wheat flour
- 1 cup bread flour
- 1 teaspoon salt
- 1 cup sourdough starter (active and bubbly)
- 1 cup lukewarm water
- Olive oil (for greasing)
- Pizza toppings of your choice (e.g., sauce, cheese, vegetables, meats)

DIRECTIONS

1. In a large mixing bowl, combine the whole wheat flour, bread flour, and salt.
2. In a separate dish, whisk together the sourdough starter and lukewarm water.
3. Pour the wet ingredients into the dry ingredients and stir until a dough forms.
4. Transfer the dough to a floured surface and knead for about 10 minutes till it becomes smooth and elastic.
5. Place the dough back into the bowl, cover, and let it rest at room temperature for 12 to 18 hours, or until it doubles in size.
6. Once the dough has risen, punch it down and divide it into two equal portions.
7. Preheat the oven to the highest temperature your oven can reach (usually around 500°F or 260°C).
8. Lightly grease two baking sheets or pizza pans with olive oil.
9. Take one portion of the dough and stretch it out on the greased baking sheet or pizza pan to form a thin crust.
10. Repeat the same process with the second portion of the dough on the other baking sheet or pizza pan.
11. Top the pizza crusts with your favorite sauce, cheese, vegetables, meats, or any desired toppings.
12. Place the baking sheets or pizza pans in the preheated oven and bake for 12 to 15 minutes, or until the crust is crispy and the toppings are cooked and golden.
13. Remove from the oven, let the pizzas cool for a few minutes, and then slice and serve.

Nutrition Value (Per Serving - 1/4 Pizza Crust): Calories: 180; Proteins: 6g; Carbs: 36g; Fats: 2g; Cholesterol: 0mg; Sodium: 230mg

12. BUTTERMILK PANCAKES

Prep Time: 15 minutes

Total Time: 12 hours (including resting and fermentation time)

Serving: Makes about 12 pancakes

INGREDIENTS

- 1 1/2 cups whole wheat flour
- 1/2 teaspoon salt
- 1 teaspoon baking powder
- 1/2 teaspoon baking soda
- 2 tablespoons sugar
- 1 cup sourdough starter (active and bubbly)
- 1 cup buttermilk
- 2 large egg
- 2 tbsps. melted butter or vegetable oil
- Optional toppings: maple syrup, fresh fruits, yogurt, etc.

DIRECTIONS

1. In a mixing dish, whisk together the whole wheat salt, baking soda, baking powder, sugar, and flour.
2. In a separate dish, whisk together the sourdough starter, buttermilk, eggs, and melted butter (or oil).
3. After adding the liquid components, mix the dry ingredients only until they are barely blended. Be careful not to over mix; a few lumps are fine.
4. Cover the bowl with a clean kitchen towel and let the batter rest at room temperature for 8 to 12 hours, or overnight. This allows the sourdough to ferment and develop flavor.
5. Preheat a griddle or a large non-stick skillet with moderate heat. Lightly grease with butter or oil.
6. Spoon about 1/4 cup of the batter onto the grill for each pancake. Cook until small bubbles form on the surface, then flip and cook the other side until golden brown.
7. Repeat with the remaining batter, adjusting the heat as necessary to prevent burning.
8. Serve the pancakes warm with your favorite toppings, such as maple syrup, fresh fruits, yogurt, or any desired accompaniments.

Nutrition Value (Per Serving - 1 Pancake): Calories: 110; Proteins: 4g; Carbs: 18g; Fats: 3g; Cholesterol: 45mg; Sodium: 240mg

13. HONEY BAGELS

Prep Time: 30 minutes

Total Time: 24 hours

Servings: Makes about 8 bagels

INGREDIENTS

- 2 cups whole wheat flour
- 1 cup bread flour
- 1 tbsp. sugar
- 1 tsp. salt
- 1 cup active and bubbly sourdough starter
- 3/4 cup lukewarm water
- 1 tbsp. honey (optional)
- Toppings of your choice (e.g., sesame seeds, poppy seeds, dried onion flakes)

DIRECTIONS

1. Mix whole wheat flour, bread flour, sugar, and salt in a bowl.
2. In a separate bowl, combine sourdough starter, lukewarm water, and honey (if using).
3. Add wet ingredients to dry ingredients and mix until a dough forms.
4. Knead the dough for 10 minutes until elastic and smooth.
5. Let the dough rise for 12-18 hours.
6. Preheat the oven to 425°F (220°C).
7. Divide the dough into 8 equal portions and shape them into bagels.
8. Boil a large pot of water and add honey (if using).
9. Boil the bagels for 1-2 minutes on each side.
10. Remove the bagels from the water and place them on a baking sheet.
11. Sprinkle desired toppings on the bagels.
12. Bake in the preheated oven for 20-25 minutes or until golden brown.
13. Let the bagels cool before slicing and serving.

Nutrition Value (Per Serving - 1 Bagel): Calories: 180; Protein: 6g; Carbs: 38g: Fat: 1g; Cholesterol: 0mg; Sodium: 280mg

CHAPTER 10
DESSERTS

1. BLUEBERRY MUFFINS

Prep Time: 15 minutes   **Total Time:** 35 minutes   **Servings:** 12 muffins

INGREDIENTS

- 2 cups flour
- 1/2 cup granulated sugar
- 1 teaspoon baking powder
- 1/2 tsp. baking soda
- 1/4 teaspoon salt
- 1 cup sourdough discard
- 1/2 cup unsalted butter, melted
- 2 large eggs
- 1 teaspoon vanilla extract
- 1 cup blueberries

DIRECTIONS

1. Preheat the oven to 375°F (190°C). Line a muffin tin with paper liners or grease the cups.
2. In a huge bowl, whip together the salt, baking soda, baking powder, sugar, and flour.
3. In another bowl, combine the sourdough discard, melted butter, eggs, as well as vanilla essence. Whisk until well blended.
4. Pour the wet ingredients into the dry ingredients and stir until just combined. Gently fold in the blueberries.
5. Spoon the pouring batter into the ready muffin tins filling each cup about 3/4 full. Bake for 18-20 minutes or when a toothpick is put into the center arrives clear.
6. Remove the muffins out of your oven let them cool in the tin for a few minutes before transferring to a wire rack to cool completely.

Nutrition Value (per serving): Calories: 198; Proteins: 4g; Carbs: 29g; Fats: 8g; Cholesterol: 51mg; Sodium: 165mg

2. CHOCOLATE CHIP COOKIES

Prep Time: 20 minutes   **Total Time:** 40 minutes   **Servings:** 24 cookies

INGREDIENTS

- 1/2 cup unsalted butter
- 1/2 cup granulated sugar
- 1/2 cup brown sugar
- 1/2 cup sourdough discard
- 1 large egg
- 1 teaspoon vanilla essence
- 1 3/4 cups flour
- 1/2 tsp. baking soda
- 1/2 teaspoon salt
- 1 cup chocolate chips

DIRECTIONS

1. Turn the oven on to 375 degrees Fahrenheit (190 degrees Celsius). Use parchment paper or a silicone mat to line a baking sheet.
2. In a mixing bowl, cream together the softened butter, sugar, and brown sugar until light and fluffy.
3. Add the sourdough discard, egg, as well as vanilla essence to the butter mixture. Mix until well combined.
4. Flour, baking powder, and salt should be mixed together in a separate bowl. Add the dry ingredients to the wet and stir until incorporated. Mix chocolate chips until evenly distributed throughout the dough.
5. Drop rounded tablespoons of dough onto the prepared baking sheet, spacing them about 2 inches apart. Bake for 10-12 minutes or until golden brown around the edges.
6. Remove the cookies out of your oven let them cool on the baking sheet for a few minutes before transferring them to a wire rack to cool completely.

Nutrition Value (per serving): Calories: 129; Proteins: 2g; Carbs: 18g; Fats: 6g; Cholesterol: 18mg; Sodium: 86mg

3. COFFEE CAKE

Prep Time: 20 minutes   **Total Time:** 1 hour   **Servings:** 9 squares

INGREDIENTS

- For the Streusel Topping:
- 1/2 cup flour
- 1/2 cup packed brown sugar
- 1/2 teaspoon ground cinnamon
- 1/4 cup unsalted butter, melted

For the Cake:
- 2 cups flour
- 1 tsp. baking powder
- 1/2 tsp. baking soda
- 1/4 teaspoon salt
- 1/2 cup unsalted butter
- 3/4 cup refined sugar
- 1/2 cup sourdough discard
- 1 large egg
- 1 teaspoon vanilla extract
- 3/4 cup milk

DIRECTIONS

1. Preheat the oven to 350°F (175°C). Grease a 9-inch square baking pan.
2. In a small bowl, prepare the streusel topping by combining the flour, brown sugar, cinnamon, and melted butter. Mix until crumbly and set aside.
3. In a separate bowl, whip together the flour, baking powder, baking soda, and salt for the cake.
4. In a mixing bowl, cream together the softened butter, refined sugar, and sourdough discard until light and fluffy.
5. Beat in the egg as well as vanilla essence until well combined. Gradually add the dry ingredients to the butter mixture, alternating with the milk, beginning and ending with the dry ingredients.
6. Pour half of the cake batter into the prepared pan. Spread half of the crumb topping on top of the batter. Layer the remaining batter and crumbs on top.
7. Bake for 30-35 minutes or when a toothpick is put into the center arrives clear. Allow the coffee cake to cool in the pan for 10 minutes before cutting it into squares and serving.

Nutrition Value (per serving): Calories: 382; Proteins: 5g; Carbs: 54g; Fats: 16g; Cholesterol: 66mg; Sodium: 181mg

4. DOUGHNUTS

Prep Time: 2 hours   **Total Time:** 3 hours   **Servings:** 12 doughnuts

INGREDIENTS

- 1 cup active sourdough starter
- 1/2 cup milk
- 1/4 cup refined sugar
- 2 tbsp. unsalted butter, melted
- 1 tsp. vanilla essence
- 2 1/2 cups flour
- 1/2tsp. salt
- 1/2tsp. ground cinnamon
- 1/4 tsp. ground nutmeg
- Vegetable oil, for frying

For the Glaze:
- 2 cups powdered sugar
- 3-4 tablespoons milk
- 1/2tsp. vanilla extract

DIRECTIONS

1. In a mixing bowl, combine the sourdough starter, milk, refined sugar, melted butter, as well as vanilla essence. Stir until well blended.
2. In a separate bowl, whip together the flour, salt, cinnamon, and nutmeg. Gradually add the dry ingredients to the sourdough mixture, stirring until a soft dough forms.
3. Turn the dough out onto a board that has been lightly dusted with flour and knead for about 5 minutes until elastic and smooth. Place the dough in a greased bowl, cover, and let it rise for 1-2 hours or until size has more than doubled.
4. Punch down the dough and roll it out to a ½ inch thickness. Use a doughnut cutter or two differently sized round cookie cutters to cut out doughnuts and doughnut holes.
5. Heat vegetable oil in a deep fryer or large pot to 375°F (190°C). Fry the doughnuts in batches, turning once, until golden brown on both sides. Drain on paper towels.
6. In a small bowl, whip together the powdered sugar, milk, as well as vanilla essence to make the glaze. Dip each doughnut into the glaze, allowing any excess to drip off. Place them on a wire rack to set.
7. Serve the sourdough doughnuts fresh and enjoy!

Nutrition Value (per serving): Calories: 278; Proteins: 4g; Carbs: 57g; Fats: 4g; Cholesterol: 9mg; Sodium: 105mg

5. BROWNIES

Prep Time: 15 minutes   **Total Time:** 40 minutes   **Servings:** 16 brownies

INGREDIENTS

- 1/2 cup unsalted butter
- 1 cup refined sugar
- 1 tsp. vanilla essence
- 2 large eggs
- 1/2 cup sourdough discard
- 1/2 cup flour
- 1/4 cup unsweetened cocoa powder
- 1/4 teaspoon salt
- 1/2 cup semisweet chocolate chips

DIRECTIONS

1. Preheat the oven to 350°F (175°C). Grease an 8x8-inch baking pan and set it aside.
2. In a microwave-safe bowl, melt the butter. Stir in the sugar as well as vanilla essence until well combined.
3. Beat in the eggs, one at a time, until fully incorporated. Add the sourdough discard and mix until smooth.
4. In a separate bowl, whip together the flour, cocoa powder, and salt. Gradually add the dry ingredients to the wet ingredients, mixing until just combined.
5. Melt the chocolate and mix it in. When the pan is ready, pour the batter inside and smooth the top.
6. Bake for 25-30 minutes or when a toothpick is put into the center comes out with a few moist crumbs.
7. Take the brownies out of the oven, then allow them to cool completely in the pan before cutting into squares and serving.

Nutrition Value (per serving): Calories: 169; Proteins: 2g; Carbs: 23g; Fats: 9g; Cholesterol: 36mg; Sodium: 51mg

6. PANCAKES

Prep Time: 10 minutes   **Total Time:** 25 minutes   **Servings:** 4 servings (about 12 pancakes)

INGREDIENTS

- 1 cup flour
- 2 tbs. refined sugar
- 1 tsp. baking powder
- 1/2 tsp. baking soda
- 1/4 teaspoon salt
- 1 cup sourdough discard
- 1/2 cup milk
- 1 large egg
- 2 tablespoons unsalted butter, melted

DIRECTIONS

1. In a huge bowl, whip together the salt, baking soda, baking powder, sugar, and flour.
2. In a separate bowl, combine the sourdough discard, milk, egg, and melted butter. Whisk until well blended.
3. Pour the wet ingredients into the dry ingredients and stir until just combined. Let the batter rest for 5 minutes.
4. Heat a lightly greased grill or non-stick skillet with moderate heat. Pour 1/4 cup of batter on the grill for each pancake.
5. Cook pancakes until bubbles form on the surface and the edges start to set, about 2-3 minutes. Flip the pancakes and cook for an additional 1-2 minutes or until golden brown.
6. Repeat with the remaining batter, adding more oil or butter to the griddle as needed.
7. Serve the sourdough pancakes warm with your favorite toppings such as maple syrup, fresh fruit, or whipped cream.

Nutrition Value (per serving): Calories: 263; Proteins: 7g; Carbs: 44g; Fats: 6g; Cholesterol: 68mg; Sodium: 446mg

7. APPLE PIE

Prep Time: 30 minutes   **Total Time:** 1 hour 30 minutes   **Servings:** 8 slices

INGREDIENTS

- For the Crust:
- 2 1/2 cups flour
- 1 teaspoon salt
- 1 teaspoon refined sugar
- 1 cup unsalted butter, cold
- 1/4 cup ice water

For the Filling:
- 4 cups peeled and sliced apples
- 1/2 cup refined sugar
- 1/4 cup flour
- 1 teaspoon ground cinnamon
- 1/4 teaspoon ground nutmeg
- 1 tablespoon lemon juice

For the Topping:
- 1/4 cup flour
- 1/4 cup packed brown sugar
- 1/4 cup rolled oats
- 2 tablespoons unsalted butter, softened

DIRECTIONS

1. In a large bowl, whip together the flour, salt and refined sugar for the crust. Add the cold butter pieces and use a pastry cutter or your fingers to cut the butter into the flour to the point that the mixture resembles crushed crumbs.
2. Gradually add the ice water, 1 tablespoon at a time, mixing with a fork after each addition. Continue adding water until the dough comes together when pressed.
3. Divide the dough in half and shape each portion into a disk. Wrap them in plastic wrap and refrigerate for at least 30 minutes.
4. Preheat the oven to 375°F (190°C). With the floured surface, roll out one dough disk to fit a 9-inch pie plate. Transfer the rolled dough to the pie plate and trim the excess.
5. Sliced apples, flour, cinnamon, nutmeg, sugar, and so on should be combined in a big basin, and lemon juice for the filling. Toss until the apples are coated.
6. Pour the apple filling into the prepared pie crust.
7. In a separate bowl, mix together the flour, brown sugar, oats, and softened butter for the topping until crumbly. Sprinkle the topping over the apple filling.
8. Cut the second dough disc into strips before rolling it out. Lay the strips out in a grid-like pattern over the pie.
9. Bake for 45-50 minutes or until the crust is golden brown and the filling is bubbling. If the edges of the crust start to brown too quickly, cover them with foil.
10. Remove the pie out of your oven let it cool for at least 1 hour before slicing and serving.

Nutrition Value (per serving): Calories: 378; Proteins: 4g; Carbs: 52g; Fats: 18g; Cholesterol: 41mg; Sodium: 293mg

8. CHOCOLATE CAKE

Prep Time: 20 minutes   **Total Time:** 1 hour   **Servings:** 12 servings

INGREDIENTS

- 1 3/4 cups flour
- 1 1/2 teaspoons baking powder
- 1 1/2 teaspoons baking soda
- 1/2 teaspoon salt
- 3/4 cup unsweetened cocoa powder
- 1 3/4 cups refined sugar
- 1/2 cup vegetable oil
- 2 large eggs
- 1 cup sourdough discard
- 1 cup hot water
- 1 teaspoon vanilla essence

DIRECTIONS

1. Preheat the oven to 350 degrees Fahrenheit (175 degrees Celsius). Coat a 9x13-inch baking pan with cooking spray and flour.
2. In a large mixing bowl, whip together the flour, baking powder, baking soda, salt, cocoa powder, and refined sugar.
3. Add the vegetable oil, eggs, sourdough discard, hot water, as well as vanilla essence to the dry ingredients. Mix until the batter is smooth and well combined.
4. Pour the batter into the prepared baking pan and smooth the top.
5. Bake for 30-35 minutes or when a toothpick is put into the center arrives clear.
6. Remove the cake out of your oven let it cool completely in the pan before slicing and serving.

Nutrition Value (per serving): Calories: 285; Proteins: 5g; Carbs: 48g; Fats: 9g; Cholesterol: 31mg; Sodium: 383mg

9. SOURDOUGH PEACH COBBLER

Prep Time: 20 minutes   **Total Time:** 1 hour 10 minutes   **Servings:** 8 servings

INGREDIENTS

- 4 cups peeled and sliced fresh peaches
- 1 cup refined sugar, divided
- 1/4 cup unsalted butter, melted
- 1 cup flour
- 1/2 cup sourdough discard
- 2 teaspoons baking powder
- 1/4 teaspoon salt
- 1/2 cup milk
- 1 teaspoon of vanilla essence
- 1/4 teaspoon ground cinnamon

DIRECTIONS

1. Preheat the oven to 350°F (175°C). Grease a 9x9-inch baking dish.
2. Inside a medium-sized bowl, combine the sliced peaches and 1/4 cup of refined sugar. Toss to coat the peaches evenly and let them sit for 10 minutes.
3. In a separate bowl, whip together the melted butter, remaining 3/4 cup of refined sugar, flour, sourdough discard, baking powder, salt, milk, as well as vanilla essence until smooth.
4. The batter should be poured into a greased baking dish. Arrange the peaches in a single layer atop the batter. Cinnamon powder goes on top.
5. Bake for 40-45 minutes or until the top is golden brown and the cobbler is bubbling around the edges.
6. Remove out of your oven let it cool for a few minutes. Serve warm with a scoop of vanilla ice cream, if desired.

Nutrition Value (per serving): Calories: 285; Proteins: 3g; Carbs: 53g; Fats: 7g; Cholesterol: 18mg; Sodium: 166mg

10. PUMPKIN BREAD

Prep Time: 15 minutes   **Total Time:** 1 hour 30 minutes   **Servings:** 12 slices

INGREDIENTS

- 1 3/4 cups flour
- 1 tsp. baking soda
- 1/2 tsp. baking powder
- 1/2 teaspoon salt
- 1 teaspoon ground cinnamon
- 1/2 tsp. ground nutmeg
- 1/4 tsp. ground cloves
- 1/2 cup refined sugar
- 1 teaspoon of vanilla essence
- 1/2 cup packed brown sugar
- 1/2 cup unsalted butter, melted
- 1 cup pumpkin puree
- 1/2 cup sourdough discard
- 2 large eggs

DIRECTIONS

1. Set the temperature to 175 degrees Celsius (or 350 degrees Fahrenheit). Prepare a 9x5-inch loaf pan with butter.
2. Inside a medium-sized bowl, whip together the flour, nutmeg, baking soda, salt, baking powder, cinnamon, and cloves. Set aside.
3. In a large bowl, combine the refined sugar, brown sugar, melted butter, pumpkin puree, sourdough discard, eggs, as well as vanilla essence. Mix well until smooth.
4. Add the dry components to the wet ones little by little and mix until everything is evenly distributed.
5. Spread the batter evenly in the prepared pan and smooth the top using a spatula.
6. Bake for 55-60 minutes or when a toothpick is put into the center arrives clear.
7. Remove out of your oven let the pumpkin bread cool in the pan for 10 minutes. Then, transfer it to a wire rack to cool completely before slicing.

Nutrition Value (per serving): Calories: 222; Proteins: 3g; Carbs: 35g; Fats: 8g; Cholesterol: 46mg; Sodium: 257mg

11. RASPBERRY TART

Prep Time: 30 minutes   **Total Time:** 2 hours 30 minutes   **Servings:** 8 slices

INGREDIENTS

- 1 1/2 cups flour
- 1/4 cup refined sugar
- 1/4 teaspoon salt
- 1/2 cup unsalted butter, cold and cubed
- 1/4 cup sourdough discard
- 2 cups fresh raspberries
- 2 tablespoons cornstarch
- 1/4 cup refined sugar
- 1 tablespoon lemon juice
- 1 teaspoon lemon zest
- Powdered sugar (for dusting)

DIRECTIONS

1. In a food processor, combine the flour, refined sugar, and salt. Add the cold cubed butter and pulse to the point that the mixture resembles crushed crumbs.
2. Add the sourdough discard and pulse a few times until the dough comes together.
3. Turn the dough out onto a lightly floured surface and shape it into a disk. Wrap in plastic wrap and refrigerate for at least 1 hour.
4. Preheat the oven to 375°F (190°C). With the floured surface, roll out the chilled dough into a circle that fits your tart pan.
5. Transfer the rolled-out dough to a greased tart pan, pressing it into the bottom and sides. Trim any excess dough.
6. In a bowl, combine the raspberries, cornstarch, refined sugar, lemon juice, and lemon zest. Gently toss to coat the raspberries.
7. Spread the raspberry mixture evenly over the tart crust.
8. Bake for 30-35 minutes or until the crust is golden brown and the raspberries are bubbling.
9. Remove out of your oven let the tart cool completely in the pan. Dust with powdered sugar before serving.

Nutrition Value (per serving): Calories: 263; Proteins: 3g; Carbs: 35g; Fats: 12g; Cholesterol: 31mg; Sodium: 63mg

12. CHERRY CLAFOUTIS

Prep Time: 15 minutes   **Total Time:** 45 minutes   **Servings:** 6 servings

INGREDIENTS

- 2 cups fresh sweet cherries, pitted
- 3/4 cup flour
- 1/2 cup refined sugar
- 1/4 teaspoon salt
- 3 large eggs
- 1 cup milk
- 1/4 cup sourdough discard
- 1 teaspoon of vanilla essence
- Powdered sugar (for dusting)

DIRECTIONS

1. Preheat the oven to 350°F (175°C). Grease a 9-inch pie dish or baking dish.
2. Arrange the pitted cherries in a single layer in the greased dish.
3. Inside a medium-sized bowl, whip together the flour, refined sugar, and salt.
4. In a separate bowl, whip together the eggs, milk, sourdough discard, as well as vanilla essence.
5. Gradually add the wet ingredients to the dry ingredients, whisking until smooth.
6. Pour the batter over the cherries in the dish.
7. Bake for 30-35 minutes or until the clafoutis is puffed and golden brown on top.
8. Remove out of your oven let it cool for a few minutes. Dust with powdered sugar before serving.

Nutrition Value (per serving): Calories: 216; Proteins: 6g; Carbs: 40g; Fats: 3g; Cholesterol: 94mg; Sodium: 118mg

13. CARROT CAKE

Prep Time: 25 minutes   **Total Time:** 1 hour 30 minutes   **Servings:** 12 servings

INGREDIENTS

- 2 cups flour
- 1 1/2 teaspoons baking powder
- 1 tsp. baking soda
- 1/2 teaspoon salt
- 1 teaspoon ground cinnamon
- 1/2 teaspoon ground nutmeg
- 1/4 teaspoon ground cloves
- 1/2 cup refined sugar
- 1/2 cup packed brown sugar
- 1/2 cup vegetable oil
- 1/2 cup sourdough discard
- 3 large eggs
- 1 teaspoon of vanilla essence
- 2 cups grated carrots
- 1/2 cup crushed pineapple, drained
- 1/2 cup shredded coconut
- 1/2 cup chopped walnuts (optional)
- Cream Cheese Frosting:
- 3 cups of powdered sugar
- 8 oz. of cream cheese, softened
- 1 teaspoon of vanilla essence
- 1/2 cup of unsalted butter

DIRECTIONS

1. Preheat the oven to 350 degrees Fahrenheit (175 degrees Celsius). Coat a 9x13-inch baking pan with cooking spray and flour.
2. Inside a medium-sized bowl, whip together the flour, nutmeg, baking powder, salt, cinnamon, baking soda, and cloves. Put aside.
3. In a large bowl, combine the refined sugar, brown sugar, vegetable oil, sourdough discard, eggs, as well as vanilla essence. Mix well until smooth.
4. Combine the wet and dry components by gradually adding the dry to the wet and stirring until just blended.
5. Fold in the grated carrots, shredded coconut, crushed pineapple, and chopped walnuts (if using).
6. Pour the mixture into the prepared baking pan and spread it evenly.
7. Bake for 30-35 minutes or when a toothpick is put into the center arrives clear.
8. Remove out of your oven let the carrot cake cool completely in the pan before frosting.
9. Cream the butter and softened cream cheese together till smooth and creamy for the cream cheese icing. Beat in the powdered sugar and vanilla extract gradually till combined.
10. Once the cake has cooled, spread the cream cheese frosting over the top. Slice and serve.

Nutrition Value (per serving): Calories: 435; Proteins: 5g; Carbs: 62g; Fats: 20g; Cholesterol: 68mg; Sodium: 373mg

14. BREAD PUDDING

Prep Time: 20 minutes   **Total Time:** 1 hour 20 minutes   **Servings:** 8 servings

INGREDIENTS

- 6 cups stale sourdough bread, cubed
- 1/2 teaspoon ground cinnamon
- 2 cups milk
- 1/2 cup heavy cream
- 1/2 cup refined sugar
- 4 large eggs
- 1 teaspoon of vanilla essence
- 1/4 teaspoon ground nutmeg
- 1/2 cup raisins (optional)
- Caramel Sauce (optional):
- 1 cup refined sugar
- 1/4 cup water
- 1/2 cup heavy cream
- 2 tablespoons unsalted butter
- 1 teaspoon of vanilla essence

DIRECTIONS

1. Preheat the oven to 350°F (175°C). Grease a 9x9-inch baking dish.
2. Place the cubed sourdough bread in the greased baking dish.
3. In a medium saucepan, heat the milk, heavy cream, and refined sugar over medium heat until hot but not boiling.
4. In a separate bowl, whip together the eggs, vanilla extract, ground cinnamon, and ground nutmeg. Slowly pour the hot milk mixture into the egg mixture, whisking constantly.
5. If using raisins, sprinkle them over the cubed bread in the baking dish.
6. Pour the milk and egg mixture over the bread, pressing down gently to ensure the bread absorbs the liquid.
7. Let the bread pudding sit for 10-15 minutes to allow the bread to soak up the liquid.
8. Bake for 45-50 minutes or until the top is golden brown and the custard is set.
9. Caramel sauce (if using) can be made while the bread pudding bakes. Mix the water and refined sugar in a sauce pan. To dissolve the sugar and bring the mixture to a boil, cook over a moderate flame, stirring often. To achieve a rich caramel hue, keep cooking without stirring. Turn off the heat and stir in the butter, heavy cream, and vanilla extract. Mix thoroughly.
10. Remove the bread pudding out of your oven let it cool for a few minutes. Serve warm with caramel sauce, if desired.

Nutrition Value (per serving): Calories: 364; Proteins: 9g; Carbs: 60g; Fats: 10g; Cholesterol: 138mg; Sodium: 259mg

15. PECAN PIE

Prep Time: 15 minutes   **Total Time:** 1 hour 15 minutes   **Servings:** 8 servings

INGREDIENTS

- 1 prepared sourdough pie crust
- 1 cup refined sugar
- 3 large eggs
- 1 cup corn syrup
- 1/4 cup unsalted butter, melted
- 1 teaspoon of vanilla essence
- 1/4 teaspoon of salt
- 1 1/2 cups pecan halves

DIRECTIONS

1. Preheat the oven to 350°F (175°C).
2. Roll out the sourdough pie crust and press it into a 9-inch pie dish.
3. In a large bowl, whip together the refined sugar, corn syrup, melted butter, eggs, vanilla extract, and salt until well combined.
4. Arrange the pecan halves in the pie crust, spreading them evenly.
5. Pour the sugar mixture over the pecans, ensuring they are fully covered.
6. Arrange a baking sheet underneath the pie to catch any overflow. The filling should be set yet somewhat puffed after 45-50 minutes in the oven.
7. Remove out of your oven let the pie cool completely before slicing.

Nutrition Value (per serving): Calories: 534; Proteins: 5g; Carbs: 80g; Fats: 24g; Cholesterol: 99mg; Sodium: 166mg

CHAPTER 11
GLUTEN-FREE

1. BAGELS

Prep Time: 30 minutes   **Total Time:** 24 hours   **Servings:** 6 bagels

INGREDIENTS

- 2 cups gluten-free sourdough starter
- 2 1/2 cups gluten-free flour blend
- 1 teaspoon salt
- 1 tablespoon honey
- 1 tsp. baking soda
- Toppings of your choice (sesame seeds, poppy seeds, etc.)

DIRECTIONS

1. Put the sourdough starter, gluten-free flour, salt, and honey into a large mixing basin. Makes a sticky dough when mixed thoroughly.
2. Split the dough in half and roll each half into a bagel shape. Line a baking sheet with parchment paper and set the items there.
3. Turn the oven temperature up to 425 degrees Fahrenheit (220 degrees Celsius).
4. Get some water boiling in a big pot. When the water is boiling, stir in the baking soda.
5. Bagels should be boiled for 1-2 minutes per side before being transferred back to the baking sheet using a slotted spoon.
6. You can top the bagels with whatever you choose.
7. Bagels need to be baked for 20-25 minutes in a preheated oven until they are golden brown and fully done.
8. Bagels should be served after being allowed to cool on a wire rack.

Nutrition Value (per bagel): Calories: 220; Proteins: 4g; Carbs: 48g; Fats: 1g; Cholesterol: 0mg; Sodium: 500mg

2. PANCAKES

Prep Time: 10 minutes   **Total Time:** 30 minutes   **Servings:** 4 servings

INGREDIENTS

- 1 cup gluten less sourdough starter
- 1 cup gluten-free flour blend
- 2 tablespoons sugar
- 1 tsp. baking powder
- 1/2tsp. baking soda
- 1/2 teaspoon salt
- 1 cup milk (dairy or plant-based)
- 2 tablespoons melted butter or oil
- 2 eggs

DIRECTIONS

1. Mix the sourdough starter with the gluten-free flour blend, sugar, baking powder, salt, and baking soda in a large mixing basin.
2. Milk, melted butter or oil, and eggs should be mixed together in a separate basin.
3. Combine the wet and dry ingredients by pouring the wet into the dry and stirring until just blended. Take ten minutes to relax while the batter sits.
4. Preheat a griddle or nonstick pan over medium heat. For each pancake, add a scant 1/4 cup of batter to the sizzling pan.
5. Fry till golden brown on one side, then flip and fry for another minute or two.
6. Pancakes should be served hot with toppings of choice.

Nutrition Value (per serving, without toppings): Calories: 280; Proteins: 8g; Carbs: 41g; Fats: 9g; Cholesterol: 100mg; Sodium: 500mg

3. PIZZA CRUST

Prep Time: 15 minutes   **Total Time:** 24 hours   **Servings:** 4 servings

INGREDIENTS

- 2 cups gluten-free sourdough starter
- 2 cups gluten-free flour blend
- 1 teaspoon salt
- 1 tablespoon olive oil
- 1/2 cup warm water
- Pizza sauce
- Cheese and toppings of your choice

DIRECTIONS

1. To make gluten-free sourdough, add a gluten-free flour blend, sourdough starter, salt, olive oil, and warm water in a large mixing basin. Stir vigorously until a dough is formed.
2. Knead the dough until it is smooth and elastic, which should take around 5 minutes.
3. Return the dough to the mixing bowl, cover with a clean kitchen towel, and let it ferment for 12 to 24 hours at room temperature.
4. Prepare a 450F (230C) oven. Pre-heat the oven with a baking stone or sheet inside.
5. The dough should be turned out onto a floured surface after the fermentation period is through. Pizza dough can be rolled out to any size or thickness.
6. Move the dough from the rolling surface to the hot baking stone or sheet carefully.
7. Cover the dough with pizza sauce, leaving a 1-inch border all the way around. Sprinkle on some cheese and toppings, if you like.
8. To make a crispy crust and melty cheese on a pizza, bake it for 15-20 minutes in a preheated oven.
9. Put it on a cooling rack for a few minutes after taking it out of the oven.

Nutrition Value (per serving): Calories: 320; Proteins: 5g; Carbs: 55g; Fats: 8g; Cholesterol: 0mg; Sodium: 500mg

4. ENGLISH MUFFINS

Prep Time: 30 minutes   **Total Time:** 2 hours 30 minutes   **Servings:** 6 English muffins

INGREDIENTS

- 1 cup gluten-less sourdough starter
- 1 1/2 cups gluten-free flour blend
- 1 teaspoon salt
- 1/2 tsp. baking soda
- 1/2 cup milk (dairy or plant-based)
- 2 tablespoons melted butter or oil
- Cornmeal (for dusting)

DIRECTIONS

1. Put the sourdough starter, gluten-free flour blend, salt, and baking soda into a large mixing basin and stir until well combined.
2. Milk and the melted fat (butter or oil) should be mixed separately.
3. Add the liquids to the dry and mix until just incorporated, being careful not to over mix. Give the batter 15 minutes to chill.
4. The griddle or skillet should be heated over medium heat. Spread some butter or oil and then sprinkle some cornmeal on the surface.
5. Make muffins in the shape of a circular biscuit cutter or a jar lid that has been oiled. Put them in the hot pan or griddle.
6. Toast the muffins for 8 to 10 minutes per side, or until golden brown and fully cooked.
7. Use a fork to make holes and crevices in the muffins. You should toast them before using.

Nutrition Value (per English muffin): Calories: 180; Proteins: 4g; Carbs: 31g; Fats: 5g; Cholesterol: 10mg; Sodium: 400mg

5. CINNAMON ROLLS

Prep Time: 30 minutes   **Total Time:** 3 hours   **Servings:** 12 rolls

INGREDIENTS

For the dough:
- 2 cups gluten-free sourdough starter
- 3 cups gluten-free flour blend
- 1/4 cup refined sugar
- 1 teaspoon salt
- 1/2 cup milk (dairy or plant-based)
- 2 tablespoons melted butter or oil
- 2 eggs

For the filling:
- 1/2 cup packed brown sugar
- 2 tablespoons ground cinnamon
- 2 tablespoons melted butter or oil

For the glaze:
- 1 cup powdered sugar
- 2 tablespoons milk (dairy or plant-based)
- 1/2 teaspoon vanilla extract

DIRECTIONS

1. In a sizable basin, whisk together the sourdough starter, flour, sugar, and salt that are all free of gluten.
2. Combine the milk, melted butter or oil, and eggs in a separate bowl and whisk to combine.
3. Add the liquids to the dry and mix until just incorporated, being careful not to over mix. For at least 15 minutes, rest the dough.
4. On a lightly floured surface, roll it into a rectangle, about 1/4 inch thick.
5. Brown sugar and ground cinnamon should be combined in a small basin for the filling.
6. Spread the melted butter or oil over the flattened out dough, then evenly sprinkle on the cinnamon sugar mixture.
7. Turn the dough onto one of the long sides and roll it up into a log. Make 12 even sections out of the log.
8. Spread the slices out evenly in a greased baking dish, making sure to leave some room between each roll.
9. Allow the rolls to rise in a warm location for 1 to 2 hours, or until they have size has more than doubled.
10. Bake at 350 degrees Fahrenheit (175 degrees Celsius) for ten minutes.
11. For 25-30 minutes in a preheated oven, the rolls should become golden and fully baked.
12. While the rolls bake, make the glaze by combining the powdered sugar, milk, and vanilla extract in a small dish and whisking until smooth.
13. Take the rolls out of the oven once they're done baking and set them on a cooling rack for a couple of minutes. Warm rolls, glaze, and drizzle.
14. While they're still warm and sticky, serve the sourdough cinnamon buns that are gluten-free.

Nutrition Value (per roll): Calories: 280; Proteins: 4g; Carbs: 50g; Fats: 7g; Cholesterol: 40mg; Sodium: 250mg

6. WAFFLES

Prep Time: 10 minutes   **Total Time:** 30 minutes   **Servings:** 4 servings (8 waffles)

INGREDIENTS

- 2 cups gluten-free sourdough starter
- 1 1/2 cups gluten-free flour blend
- 2 tablespoons sugar
- 1tsp. baking powder
- 1/2 tsp. baking soda
- 1/2 teaspoon salt
- 1 cup milk (dairy or plant-based)
- 2 tablespoons melted butter or oil
- 2 eggs

DIRECTIONS

1. Put the sourdough starter, gluten-free flour mixture, sugar, baking powder, salt, and baking soda into a large mixing basin.
2. Milk, melted butter or oil, and eggs should be mixed together in a separate basin.
3. Combine the wet and dry ingredients by pouring the wet into the dry and stirring until just blended. Take ten minutes to relax while the batter sits.
4. To make waffles, heat your waffle iron as directed.
5. Spread the batter evenly over the hot waffle maker. Cook the waffles with the lid closed until they are brown and crispy.
6. Keep cooking waffles until all the batter is used.
7. Waffles made from gluten-free sourdough should be served hot with toppings of choice.

Nutrition Value (per serving, 2 waffles): Calories: 380; Proteins: 8g; Carbs: 60g; Fats: 12g; Cholesterol: 120mg; Sodium: 550mg

7. TORTILLAS

Prep Time: 15 minutes   **Total Time:** 1 hour 30 minutes   **Serving:** Makes 12 tortillas

INGREDIENTS

- 2 cups gluten-free flour
- 1 teaspoon xanthan gum
- 1/2 teaspoon salt
- 1/2 cup gluten-free sourdough starter
- 1/4 cup warm water
- 2 tablespoons olive oil

DIRECTIONS

1. Combine the gluten-free flour, xanthan gum, and salt in a large mixing basin and whisk to combine.
2. All you have to do is combine the dry ingredients with the sourdough starter, some warm water, and some olive oil. Stir vigorously until a dough is formed.
3. To make an elastic and smooth dough, knead it on a lightly floured surface for about 5 minutes.
4. The dough should be cut into 12 pieces and rolled into balls.
5. Use a rolling pin to flatten each ball into a thin tortilla.
6. Preheat a griddle or skillet without nonstick coating over medium heat.
7. To ensure that each tortilla is fully cooked and has a light brown color, fry it for about a minute on each side.
8. Continue with the other spheres of dough.
9. Warm the gluten-free sourdough tortillas and use them as a foundation for your favorite toppings and meals.

Nutrition Value (per tortilla): Calories: 120; Proteins: 2g; Carbs: 20g; Fats: 3g; Cholesterol: 0mg; Sodium: 150mg

8. BAGUETTES

Prep Time: 30 minutes

Total Time: 6 hours 30 minutes
(including rising time)

Serving: Makes 2 baguettes

INGREDIENTS

- 2 cups gluten-free flour
- 1/2 cup brown rice flour
- 1/2 cup flour of tapioca
- 1 teaspoon xanthan gum
- 1 teaspoon salt
- 1/2 cup gluten-free sourdough starter
- 1 cup warm water
- 2 tablespoons olive oil

DIRECTIONS

1. In a sizable dish, whisk together the gluten-free flour, brown rice flour, tapioca flour, xanthan gum, and salt.
2. In a large bowl, combine the dry ingredients. Add the sourdough starter, and olive oil with water.
3. Knead it together until it becomes a sticky dough.
4. Cover the basin with a clean kitchen towel and let it in a warm spot to rise until the dough has size has more than doubled, about 4 hours.
5. Bake at 425 degrees Fahrenheit (220 degrees Celsius) with a baking sheet lined with parchment paper.
6. Turn the dough out onto a clean, gluten-free floured surface. Cut the dough in half so that each half is the same size.
7. Form each piece into a baguette and place on the prepared baking sheet.
8. Cut the tops of the baguettes in a diagonal pattern with a sharp knife.
9. The baguettes should be baked in a preheated oven for 30 to 35 minutes, or until golden brown and crusty, and then taken out to cool on a wire rack before being sliced and served.

Nutrition Value (per baguette): Calories: 300; Proteins: 4g; Carbs: 60g; Fats: 6g; Cholesterol: 0mg; Sodium: 350mg

9. FOCACCIA

Prep Time: 20 minutes

Total Time: 4 hours 30 minutes
(including rising time)

Serving: Makes 8 servings

INGREDIENTS

- 2 cups gluten-free flour
- 1/2 cup brown rice flour
- 1/2 cup flour of tapioca
- 1 teaspoon xanthan gum
- 1 teaspoon salt
- 1/2 cup gluten-free sourdough starter
- 1 cup warm water
- 1/4 cup olive oil
- 2 tablespoons fresh rosemary, chopped
- Coarse sea salt, for topping

DIRECTIONS

1. Sift the gluten-free flour, brown rice flour, tapioca flour, xanthan gum, and salt into a large mixing bowl.
2. To the dry ingredients, incorporate the sourdough starter, hot water, and 2 teaspoons of olive oil. Combine thoroughly so that a tacky dough forms.
3. Cover the basin with a clean kitchen towel and set it in a warm spot to rise until the dough has size has more than doubled, about 3 hours.
4. Get a baking sheet ready and turn the oven on to 425 degrees Fahrenheit (220 degrees Celsius).
5. Put the dough on the baking sheet and carefully pat it into a rectangle when it has risen.
6. Add the remaining 2 tablespoons of olive oil, along with the chopped rosemary and coarse sea salt, to the dough and rub it all together.
7. To equally distribute the oil, rosemary, and salt, push dimples into the dough with your fingertips.
8. Put in an oven that has been prepared to 350 degrees and bake for 25 to 30 minutes, or until golden brown and fully done.
9. Put it on a cooling rack for a few minutes after taking it out of the oven.

Nutrition Value (per serving): Calories: 220; Proteins: 3g; Carbs: 38g; Fats: 7g; Cholesterol: 0mg; Sodium: 300mg

10. CRACKERS

Prep Time: 15 minutes   **Total Time:** 1 hour 30 minutes   **Serving:** Makes about 40 crackers

INGREDIENTS

- 1 cup gluten-free all-purpose flour
- 1/4 cup brown rice flour
- 1/4 cup flour of tapioca
- 1/2 teaspoon xanthan gum
- 1/2 teaspoon salt
- 1/2 cup gluten-free sourdough starter
- 2 tablespoons olive oil
- 1/4 cup water
- Optional toppings: sesame seeds, poppy seeds, dried herbs, etc.

DIRECTIONS

1. Sift the gluten-free all-purpose flour, brown rice flour, flour of tapioca, xanthan gum, and salt into a large mixing bowl.
2. To the dry ingredients, include the olive oil, water, and sourdough starter. Combine thoroughly so that a dough may be formed.
3. The dough should be cut in half and rolled into two balls. Refrigerate them in a sealed plastic bag for an hour.
4. Bake at 350 degrees Fahrenheit (175 degrees Celsius) with a baking sheet lined with parchment paper.
5. Remove one dough ball from the fridge and sandwich it between two pieces of waxed paper. Flatten the dough into a thin layer, about 1/8 of an inch.
6. The dough should be rolled out, the top parchment paper removed, and then placed on the baking sheet.
7. Cut the dough into the appropriate cracker shape and size using a pizza cutter or a sharp knife.
8. Take a second ball of dough and go back over steps 5-7 again.
9. The crackers can be topped with sesame seeds, poppy seeds, or dried herbs.
10. To make crackers, place them on a baking sheet and into a preheated oven for 15-20 minutes, or until they are a golden brown and crispy.
11. Take them out of the oven and let them cool before putting them in a sealed container.

Nutrition Value (per serving, about 4 crackers): Calories: 90; Proteins: 1g; Carbs: 13g; Fats: 4g; Cholesterol: 0mg; Sodium: 100mg

11. PRETZELS

Prep Time: 30 minutes   **Total Time:** 2 hours 30 minutes (including rising time)   **Serving:** Makes 8 pretzels

INGREDIENTS

- 2 cups gluten-free flour
- 1/2 cup brown rice flour
- 1/2 cup flour of tapioca
- 1 teaspoon xanthan gum
- 1 teaspoon salt
- 1/2 cup gluten-free sourdough starter
- 1 cup warm water
- 2 tablespoons baking soda
- Coarse sea salt, for topping
- Optional: melted butter for brushing

DIRECTIONS

1. In a large mixing bowl, combine the gluten-free flour, brown rice flour, flour of tapioca, xanthan gum, and salt.
2. Add the sourdough starter and warm water to the dry ingredients. Mix well until a soft dough forms.
3. Cover the bowl with a clean kitchen towel and let the dough rise in a warm place for about 2 hours, until it doubles in size.
4. Preheat the oven to 425°F (220°C) and use parchment paper to cover a baking sheet.
5. Divide the risen dough into 8 equal portions.
6. Roll each portion of dough into a long rope, about 20 inches in length.
7. Shape each rope into a pretzel shape, twisting the ends to secure.
8. In a large pot, bring water to a boil. Add the baking soda to the boiling water.
9. Carefully drop the pretzels into the boiling water, one or two at a time, and let them boil for about 30 seconds. Remove with a slotted spoon and place them on the prepared baking sheet.
10. Sprinkle coarse sea salt over the pretzels.
11. Bake in the preheated oven for 12-15 minutes, or until the pretzels are golden brown.
12. Optional: Brush the pretzels with melted butter for a glossy finish.
13. Remove out of your oven let them cool slightly before serving.

Nutrition Value (per pretzel): Calories: 180; Proteins: 2g; Carbs: 38g; Fats: 2g; Cholesterol: 0mg; Sodium: 800mg

12. DONUTS

Prep Time: 30 minutes   **Total Time:** 3 hours (including rising and frying time)   **Serving:** Makes 12 donuts

INGREDIENTS

- 2 cups gluten-free flour
- 1/2 cup brown rice flour
- 1/2 cup flour of tapioca
- 1 teaspoon xanthan gum
- 1/2 teaspoon salt
- 1/2 cup gluten-free sourdough starter
- 1/2 cup warm milk (or dairy-free alternative)
- 1/4 cup sugar
- 2 tablespoons melted butter (or dairy-free alternative)
- 2 teaspoons vanilla extract
- 2 large eggs
- Oil, for frying (such as vegetable or canola oil)
- Optional toppings: powdered sugar, cinnamon sugar, glaze, sprinkles, etc.

DIRECTIONS

1. In a large mixing bowl, combine the gluten- flour, brown rice flour, flour of tapioca, xanthan gum, and salt.
2. In a separate bowl, mix together the sourdough starter, warm milk, sugar, melted butter, vanilla extract, and eggs.
3. Pour the wet ingredients into the dry ingredients and mix until well combined, forming a soft dough.
4. Cover the bowl with a clean kitchen towel and let the dough rise in a warm place for about 2 hours, until it doubles in size.
5. Heat oil in a large pot or deep fryer to 350°F (175°C).
6. Dust a clean surface with gluten-free flour and gently roll out the dough to about 1/2-inch thickness.
7. Use a donut cutter or a round cookie cutter to cut out donut shapes. If using a cookie cutter, make a smaller hole in the center to form the donut shape.
8. Carefully drop the donuts into the hot oil, frying them for about 2-3 minutes per side, until golden brown.
9. Remove the fried donuts with a slotted spoon and place them on a paper towel-lined plate to drain excess oil.
10. Optional: While the donuts are still warm, coat them in powdered sugar, cinnamon sugar, glaze, or sprinkles.
11. Let the donuts cool slightly before serving.

Nutrition Value (per donut): Calories: 220; Proteins: 3g; Carbs: 36g; Fats: 7g; Cholesterol: 35mg; Sodium: 180mg

13. DINNER ROLLS

Prep Time: 20 minutes

Total Time: 3 hours (including rising and baking time)

Serving: Makes 12 rolls

INGREDIENTS

- 2 cups gluten-free flour
- 1/2 cup brown rice flour
- 1/2 cup flour of tapioca
- 1 teaspoon xanthan gum
- 1 teaspoon salt
- 1/2 cup gluten-free sourdough starter
- 1 cup warm milk (or dairy-free alternative)
- 2 tablespoons melted butter (or dairy-free alternative)
- 2 tablespoons honey (or maple syrup for vegan option)
- 2 teaspoons active dry yeast
- 2 large eggs, beaten

DIRECTIONS

1. In a large mixing bowl, combine the gluten-free flour, brown rice flour, flour of tapioca, xanthan gum, and salt.
2. In a separate bowl, mix together the sourdough starter, warm milk, melted butter, honey, and active dry yeast. Let it sit for 5 minutes until the yeast activates and becomes foamy.
3. Pour the yeast mixture and beaten eggs into the dry ingredients. Mix well until a sticky dough forms.
4. Cover the bowl with a clean kitchen towel and let the dough rise in a warm place for about 2 hours, until it doubles in size.
5. Preheat the oven to 350 degrees Fahrenheit (175 degrees Celsius). Coat a 9x13-inch baking pan with cooking spray and flour.
6. Punch down the risen dough and divide it into 12 equal portions.
7. Shape each portion into a smooth ball and place them in the greased baking dish, evenly spaced.
8. Cover the baking dish with the kitchen towel and let the rolls rise for an additional 30 minutes.
9. Bake in the preheated oven for 18-20 minutes, or until the rolls are golden brown and cooked through.
10. Remove out of your oven let them cool slightly before serving.

Nutrition Value (per roll): Calories: 180; Proteins: 4g; Carbs: 32g; Fats: 4g; Cholesterol: 40mg; Sodium: 250mg

14. CAKES

Prep Time: 20 minutes

Total Time: Varies depending on cake type.

Serving: Varies depending on cake size

INGREDIENTS

- 2 cups gluten-free flour
- 1/2 cup brown rice flour
- 1/2 cup flour of tapioca
- 1 teaspoon xanthan gum
- 1 teaspoon baking powder
- 1/2 tsp. baking soda
- 1/2 teaspoon salt
- 1/2 cup gluten-free sourdough starter
- 1 cup milk (or dairy-free alternative)
- 1 cup sugar
- 1/2 cup melted butter (or dairy-free alternative)
- 2 teaspoons vanilla extract
- 3 large eggs

DIRECTIONS

1. Preheat the oven to the temperature specified in your chosen cake recipe.
2. In a large mixing bowl, combine the gluten-free flour, brown rice flour, tapioca flour, xanthan gum, baking powder, baking soda, and salt.
3. In a separate bowl, mix together the sourdough starter, milk, sugar, melted butter, vanilla extract, and eggs. Mix until well combined.
4. Pour the wet ingredients into the dry ingredients. Mix well until a smooth batter forms.
5. Follow the specific instructions of your chosen cake recipe for greasing and preparing the cake pans.
6. Pour the batter into the prepared cake pans and smooth the tops with a spatula.
7. Bake in the preheated oven for the time specified in your chosen cake recipe, or when a toothpick is put into the center arrives clear.
8. Remove out of your oven let the cakes cool completely before frosting or serving.

Nutrition Value: Calories: 350; Fat: 15 grams; Carbohydrates: 70 grams; Protein: 6 grams; Cholesterol: 70 milligrams; Sodium: 400 milligrams

15. FLATBREAD

Prep Time: 20 minutes

Total Time: 1 hour (including rising and cooking time)

Serving: Makes 4-6 flatbreads

INGREDIENTS

- 2 cups gluten-free flour
- 1 teaspoon xanthan gum
- 1 teaspoon salt
- 1/2 cup gluten-free sourdough starter
- 1/2 cup warm water
- 2 tablespoons olive oil

DIRECTIONS

1. In a large mixing bowl, combine the gluten-free all-purpose flour, xanthan gum, and salt.
2. Add the gluten-free sourdough starter and warm water to the dry ingredients. Mix well until a soft dough forms.
3. Knead the dough for a few minutes till it becomes smooth and elastic.
4. Divide the dough into 4-6 equal portions and shape them into balls.
5. On a lightly floured surface, roll out each dough ball into a thin circle or oval shape, about 1/4 inch thick.
6. Heat a non-stick skillet or griddle over medium heat. Brush the surface with olive oil.
7. Place one flatbread onto the heated skillet and cook for about 2-3 minutes on each side, or until golden brown and cooked through. Repeat with the remaining flatbreads.
8. Remove from the skillet and let them cool slightly before serving.

Nutrition Value (per flatbread): Calories: 220; Proteins: 4g; Carbs: 38g; Fats: 5g; Cholesterol: 0mg; Sodium: 400mg

16. BISCUITS

Prep Time: 15 minutes   **Total Time:** 35 minutes   **Serving:** Makes 8 biscuits

INGREDIENTS

- 1 ½ cups gluten-free flour
- 1 ½ teaspoons baking powder
- ½ tsp. baking soda
- ½ teaspoon salt
- ¼ cup cold unsalted butter (or dairy-free alternative), cubed
- ½ cup gluten-free sourdough starter
- ½ cup buttermilk (or dairy-free alternative)
- 1 tablespoon honey (or maple syrup for vegan option)

DIRECTIONS

1. Preheat the oven to 425°F (220°C) and use parchment paper to cover a baking sheet.
2. In a large mixing dish, whisk together the gluten-free all-purpose flour, baking powder, baking soda, and salt.
3. Add the cold cubed butter to the flour mixture. Use a pastry cutter or your fingers to cut the butter into the flour to the point that the mixture resembles crushed crumbs.
4. In a separate bowl, combine the gluten-free sourdough starter, buttermilk, and honey.
5. Pour the wet ingredients into the dry ingredients. Stir until just combined, being careful not to over mix.
6. Extend the dough over a lightly dusted surface. Once the dough comes together, gently knead it a few times.
7. Pat the dough into a circle or rectangle, about 1-inch thick.
8. Use a biscuit cutter or a round cookie cutter to cut out biscuits from the dough. Place them onto the prepared baking sheet, leaving a small space between each biscuit.
9. Gather the remaining dough scraps, pat them together, and cut out more biscuits until all the dough is used.
10. Bake in the preheated oven for 15-18 minutes, or until the biscuits are golden brown on top.
11. Remove out of your oven let the biscuits cool slightly before serving.

Nutrition Value (per biscuit): Calories: 180; Proteins: 3g; Carbs: 26g; Fats: 7g; Cholesterol: 20mg; Sodium: 400mg

17. PITA BREAD

Prep Time: 30 minutes

Total Time: 2 hours (including rising and cooking time)

Serving: Makes 8 pitas

INGREDIENTS

- 2 cups gluten-free all-purpose flour
- 1 teaspoon xanthan gum
- 1 teaspoon salt
- 1/2 cup gluten-free sourdough starter
- 1/2 cup warm water
- 1 tablespoon olive oil
- Additional flour for dusting

DIRECTIONS

1. In a large mixing bowl, combine the gluten-free all-purpose flour, xanthan gum, and salt.
2. Add the gluten-free sourdough starter and warm water to the dry ingredients. Mix well until a soft dough forms.
3. Knead the dough for a few minutes till it becomes smooth and elastic.
4. Divide the dough into 8 equal portions and shape them into balls.
5. On a lightly floured surface, roll out each dough ball into a thin circle, about 1/4 inch thick.
6. Place the rolled-out pitas on a baking sheet lined with parchment paper. Cover them with a clean kitchen towel and let them rise in a warm place for about 1 hour, until slightly puffed.
7. Preheat the oven to 475°F (245°C). Place a baking stone or baking sheet in the oven to preheat as well.
8. Carefully transfer the risen pitas onto the preheated baking stone or baking sheet. Bake for 6-8 minutes, or until puffed and lightly golden.
9. Remove out of your oven let the pitas cool slightly before serving.

Nutrition Value (per pita): Calories: 150; Proteins: 3g; Carbs: 32g; Fats: 2g; Cholesterol: 0mg; Sodium: 300mg

18. CINNAMON BREAD

Prep Time: 30 minutes

Total Time: 3 hours (including rising and baking time)

Serving: Makes 1 loaf

INGREDIENTS

- 2 cups gluten-free all-purpose flour
- 1/2 cup brown rice flour
- 1/2 cup tapioca flour
- 1 teaspoon xanthan gum
- 1 1/2 teaspoons ground cinnamon
- 1/2 teaspoon baking powder
- 1/2 tsp. baking soda
- 1/2 teaspoon salt
- 1/2 cup gluten-free sourdough starter
- 1/2 cup milk (or dairy-free alternative)
- 1/3 cup melted butter (or dairy-free alternative)
- 1/2 cup sugar
- 2 large eggs
- 1 teaspoon vanilla extract
- **For the cinnamon swirl:**
- 1/4 cup sugar
- 1 tablespoon ground cinnamon

DIRECTIONS

1. In a large mixing bowl, whip together the gluten-free all-purpose flour, brown rice flour, tapioca flour, xanthan gum, ground cinnamon, baking powder, baking soda, and salt.
2. In a separate bowl, mix together the gluten-free sourdough starter, milk, melted butter, sugar, eggs, as well as vanilla essence. Mix until well combined.
3. Pour the wet ingredients into the dry ingredients. Stir until just combined, being careful not to over mix.
4. Grease a 9x5-inch loaf pan and pour half of the batter into the pan.
5. In a small bowl, mix together the sugar and ground cinnamon for the cinnamon swirl.
6. Sprinkle half of the cinnamon swirl mixture over the batter in the loaf pan.
7. Pour the remaining batter on top and sprinkle the remaining cinnamon swirl mixture over the batter.
8. Use a butter knife to gently swirl the batter and cinnamon mixture together.
9. Cover the loaf pan with a clean kitchen towel and let the bread rise in a warm place for about 1-2 hours, until it reaches the top of the pan.
10. Preheat the oven to 350°F (175°C). Bake the bread for 40-45 minutes, or when a toothpick is put into the center arrives clear.
11. Remove out of your oven let the bread cool in the pan for 10 minutes. Then transfer it to a wire rack to cool completely before slicing.

Nutrition Value (per slice): Calories: 180; Proteins: 3g; Carbs: 27g; Fats: 7g; Cholesterol: 45mg; Sodium: 200mg

19. NAAN BREAD

Prep Time: 20 minutes | **Total Time:** 2 hours 30 minutes (including rising and cooking time) | **Serving:** Makes 8 naan breads

INGREDIENTS

- 2 cups gluten-free all-purpose flour
- 1 teaspoon xanthan gum
- 1 teaspoon baking powder
- 1/2tsp.baking soda
- 1/2 teaspoon salt
- 1/2 cup gluten-free sourdough starter
- 1/2 cup plain yogurt (or dairy-free alternative)
- 2 tablespoons melted butter (or dairy-free alternative)
- 1 tablespoon honey (or maple syrup for vegan option)
- 1/4 cup warm water
- **For brushing:**
- 2 tablespoons melted butter (or dairy-free alternative)
- Chopped fresh cilantro (optional)

DIRECTIONS

1. In a large mixing bowl, whip together the gluten-free all-purpose flour, xanthan gum, baking powder, baking soda, and salt.
2. In a separate bowl, mix together the gluten-free sourdough starter, yogurt, melted butter, honey, and warm water. Mix until well combined.
3. Pour the wet ingredients into the dry ingredients. Stir until a soft dough forms.
4. Knead the dough in the bowl for a few minutes till it becomes smooth and elastic.
5. Cover the bowl with a clean kitchen towel and let the dough rise in a warm place for about 1-2 hours, until it doubles in size.
6. Preheat a skillet or griddle over medium heat.
7. Divide the risen dough into 8 equal portions and shape them into balls.
8. On a lightly floured surface, roll out each dough ball into an oval or round shape, about 1/4 inch thick.
9. Place one rolled-out naan bread onto the preheated skillet or griddle. Cook for about 2 minutes on each side, or until golden brown spots appear.
10. Repeat with the remaining dough portions.
11. Brush each cooked naan bread with melted butter and sprinkle with chopped fresh cilantro, if desired.
12. Serve the naan breads warm.

Nutrition Value (per naan bread): Calories: 180; Proteins: 4g; Carbs: 30g; Fats: 5g; Cholesterol: 15mg; Sodium: 350mg

20. FRENCH TOAST

Prep Time: 10 minutes | **Total Time:** 25 minutes | **Serving:** Serves 4

INGREDIENTS

- 8 slices gluten-free sourdough bread
- 4 large eggs
- 1/2 cup milk (or dairy-free alternative)
- 1 teaspoon vanilla extract
- 1/2 teaspoon ground cinnamon
- 1 tablespoon butter (or dairy-free alternative)
- Maple syrup and fresh fruits for serving

DIRECTIONS

1. In a shallow bowl, whip together the eggs, milk, vanilla extract, and ground cinnamon until well combined.
2. Heat a large skillet or griddle over medium heat. Add the butter and let it melt.
3. Coat both sides of each piece of non-gluten- sourdough bread with the egg mixture, then set aside.
4. Place the dipped bread slices onto the heated skillet or griddle. Cook for 2-3 minutes on each side, or until golden brown and cooked through.
5. Repeat with the remaining bread slices.
6. Serve the gluten-free sourdough French toast warm with maple syrup and fresh fruits.
7. Note: You can customize the toppings for your French toast by adding sliced bananas, berries, or a sprinkle of powdered sugar. Adjust the toppings based on your preference.

Nutrition Value (per serving): Calories: 300; Proteins: 10g; Carbs: 40g; Fats: 10g; Cholesterol: 200mg; Sodium: 300mg

21. CORNBREAD

Prep Time: 10 minutes   **Total Time:** 35 minutes   **Serving:** Serves 8

INGREDIENTS

- 1 cup gluten-free cornmeal
- 1 cup gluten-free all-purpose flour
- 1/4 cup sugar
- 1 tablespoon of baking powder
- 1/2 cup gluten-free sourdough starter
- 1/2 teaspoon of salt
- 1/2 cup milk (or dairy-free alternative)
- 1/4 cup melted butter (or dairy-free alternative)
- 2 large eggs

DIRECTIONS

1. Preheat the oven to 400°F (200°C). Grease an 8-inch square baking dish or cast-iron skillet.
2. In a large mixing bowl, whip together the cornmeal, all-purpose flour, sugar, baking powder, and salt.
3. In a separate bowl, mix together the sourdough starter, milk, melted butter, and eggs. Mix until well combined.
4. Pour the wet ingredients into the dry ingredients. Stir until just combined, being careful not to over mix.
5. Pour the batter into the greased baking dish or skillet, spreading it evenly.
6. Bake in the preheated oven for 20-25 minutes, or when a toothpick is put into the center arrives clear and the top is golden brown.
7. Remove out of your oven let the cornbread cool slightly before serving.

Nutrition Value (per serving): Calories: 200; Proteins: 4g; Carbs: 30g; Fats: 7g; Cholesterol: 55mg; Sodium: 300mg

22. SANDWICH BREAD

Prep Time: 20 minutes   **Total Time:** 4 hours (including rising and baking time)   **Serving:** Makes 1 loaf

INGREDIENTS

- 2 cups gluten-free all-purpose flour
- 1 cup brown rice flour
- 1/2 cup tapioca flour
- 2 teaspoons xanthan gum
- 1 1/2 teaspoons salt
- 1/2 cup gluten-free sourdough starter
- 1 cup warm water
- 2 tablespoons honey (or maple syrup for vegan option)
- 2 tablespoons olive oil
- 2 large eggs

DIRECTIONS

1. In a large mixing bowl, whip together the gluten-free all-purpose flour, brown rice flour, tapioca flour, xanthan gum, and salt.
2. In a separate bowl, mix together the sourdough starter, warm water, honey, olive oil, and eggs. Mix until well combined.
3. Pour the wet ingredients into the dry ingredients. Stir until a sticky dough forms.
4. Grease a 9x5-inch loaf pan and transfer the dough into the pan, smoothing the top with a spatula.
5. Cover the pan with a clean kitchen towel and let the bread rise in a warm place for about 2-3 hours, until it reaches the top of the pan.
6. Preheat the oven to 375°F (190°C).
7. Bake the bread in the preheated oven for 50-60 minutes, or until golden brown on top and a toothpick inserted into the center arrives clear.
8. Remove out of your oven let the bread cool in the pan for 10 minutes. Then transfer it to a wire rack to cool completely before slicing.

Nutrition Value (per slice): Calories: 180; Proteins: 4g; Carbs: 30g; Fats: 5g; Cholesterol: 35mg; Sodium: 300mg

23. MUFFINS

Prep Time: 15 minutes   **Total Time:** 35 minutes   **Serving:** Makes 12 muffins

INGREDIENTS

- 2 cups gluten-free all-purpose flour
- 1 teaspoon xanthan gum
- 1 teaspoon baking powder
- 1/2 tsp. baking soda
- 1/4 teaspoon salt
- 1/2 cup sugar
- 1/2 cup gluten-free sourdough starter
- 1/2 cup milk (or dairy-free alternative)
- 1/4 cup melted butter (or dairy-free alternative)
- 2 large eggs
- 1 teaspoon vanilla extract
- 1 cup fresh or frozen berries (blueberries, raspberries, or strawberries)

DIRECTIONS

1. Preheat the oven to 375°F (190°C). Grease a muffin tin or line it with paper liners.
2. In a large mixing bowl, whip together the gluten-free all-purpose flour, xanthan gum, baking powder, baking soda, salt, and sugar.
3. In a separate bowl, mix together the sourdough starter, milk, melted butter, eggs, as well as vanilla essence. Mix until well combined.
4. Pour the wet ingredients into the dry ingredients. Stir until just combined.
5. Gently fold in the berries into the batter.
6. Spoon the pouring batter into the ready muffin tins filling each cup about 2/3 full.
7. Bake in the preheated oven for 18-20 minutes, or when a toothpick is put into the center of a muffin arrives clear.
8. Remove out of your oven let the muffins cool in the tin for 5 minutes. Then transfer them to a wire rack to cool completely.

Nutrition Value (per muffin): Calories: 180; Proteins: 3g; Carbs: 30g; Fats: 6g; Cholesterol: 40mg; Sodium: 200mg

Thank you from the bottom of my heart
for choosing to read this book!

It is with immense gratitude that I address these words to you. It gives me enormous pleasure to know that you have decided to give your time and attention to these pages that I have written with commitment and dedication.

Creating this book has been an exciting journey, and my hope is that you have found it as enjoyable and inspiring to read as I have in writing it. Every word was carefully chosen with the goal of conveying a message, a story or a new perspective to you.

I am aware that you have a multitude of choices available to you when it comes to books, and the fact that you chose mine is a source of great pride and happiness. Your choice is invaluable to me, as it is the support and interest of readers like you that give meaning to my work as a writer.

If you have enjoyed the journey you have taken with these pages, I kindly ask you to **share your experience with others**. Reader reviews are a vital tool for raising awareness of a book and helping other readers make an informed choice.

If you feel inspired to do so, you might **take a few minutes to write a positive review** in which you could share your opinions. Even a few words can make a huge difference and help introduce the book to a wider audience.

CHAPTER 12
SOURDOUGH DISCARD RECIPES

1. PANCAKES

Prep Time: 10 minutes   **Total Time:** 30 minutes   **Servings:** 4

INGREDIENTS

- 1 cup sourdough discard
- 1 cup flour
- 1 tablespoon sugar
- 1 teaspoon of baking powder
- 1/4 teaspoon salt
- 1 cup milk
- 1/2 tsp. of baking soda
- 1 egg
- 2 tablespoons melted butter
- Additional butter or oil for cooking

DIRECTIONS

1. In a huge bowl, combine the sourdough discard, salt, baking soda, baking powder, sugar, and flour.
2. In a separate bowl, whip together the milk, egg, and melted butter.
3. • After adding the wet ingredients, mix the dry ingredients only until they are barely incorporated. A lumpy batter is possible.
4. Heat a griddle or non-stick skillet with moderate heat and melt a small amount of butter or oil.
5. Pour 1/4 cup portions of batter onto the griddle and cook until bubbles form on the surface.
6. Flip the pancakes and cook for another 1-2 minutes, or until golden brown.
7. Serve the pancakes warm with your favorite toppings.

Nutrition Value (per serving): Calories: 250; Proteins: 8g; Carbs: 36g; Fats: 8g; Cholesterol: 60mg; Sodium: 400mg

2. WAFFLES

Prep Time: 10 minutes   **Total Time:** 25 minutes   **Servings:** 4

INGREDIENTS

- 1 1/2 cups sourdough discard
- 1/2 tsp. of baking soda
- 1 3/4 cups flour
- 2 tablespoons sugar
- 1 teaspoon of baking powder
- 1/4 teaspoon salt
- 2/3 cup milk
- 2 eggs
- 1/4 cup melted butter

DIRECTIONS

1. In a huge bowl, combine the sourdough discard, salt, baking soda, baking powder, sugar, and flour.
2. In a separate bowl, whip together the milk, eggs, and melted butter.
3. Mix wet ingredients and dry ingredients and stir until just combined. The batter may be lumpy.
4. Preheat your waffle iron according to the manufacturer's instructions.
5. Spoon the batter onto the waffle iron that has been preheated and cook until crisp and golden brown.
6. Serve the waffles warm with your favorite toppings.

Nutrition Value (per serving): Calories: 320; Proteins: 9g; Carbs: 47g; Fats: 11g; Cholesterol: 110mg; Sodium: 550mg

3. BANANA BREAD

Prep Time: 15 minutes   **Total Time:** 1 hour 15 minutes   **Servings:** 8

INGREDIENTS

- 1 1/2 cups mashed ripe bananas (about 3-4 bananas)
- 1 cup sourdough discard
- 1/2 cup granulated sugar
- 1 tsp. of baking soda
- 1/2 cup packed brown sugar
- 1/3 cup vegetable oil
- 2 eggs
- 1/2 teaspoon of ground cinnamon
- 1 tsp. of vanilla extract
- 1 3/4 cups of all-purpose flour
- 1/2 teaspoon of salt

DIRECTIONS

1. Preheat your oven at 350°F (175°C) and grease a 9x5-inch bread pan.
2. In a huge bowl, combine the mashed bananas, sourdough discard, refined sugar, brown sugar, oil, eggs, as well as vanilla essence. Mix well.
3. In a separate bowl, whip together the flour, salt, baking soda, and cinnamon.
4. Gradually put the dry components to the banana mixture, stirring until just combined.
5. Pour the batter into the prepared loaf pan and smooth the top.
6. Bake for 55-65 minutes, or when a toothpick is put into the center arrives clear.
7. Allow the banana bread to cool in the pan for 10 minutes, then transfer it to a wire rack to cool completely.

Nutrition Value (per serving): Calories: 310; Proteins: 5g; Carbs: 53g; Fats: 10g; Cholesterol: 35mg; Sodium: 310mg

4. PIZZA DOUGH

Prep Time: 10 minutes   **Total Time:** 2 hours 30 minutes   **Servings:** 4

INGREDIENTS

- 1 cup sourdough discard
- 2 1/2 cups bread flour
- 1 teaspoon salt
- 1 tablespoon olive oil

DIRECTIONS

1. In a huge bowl, combine the sourdough discard, bread flour, and salt.
2. Mix until the dough comes together, then transfer it to a floured surface.
3. Knead the dough for about 5 minutes, or till it becomes smooth and elastic.
4. Place the dough inside a greased dish and cover it with a clean kitchen towel. Let it rise at the room temperature for 2 hours.
5. Preheat your oven at the highest temperature it can reach.
6. Divide the dough into 4 portions and shape them into balls. Let them rest for 10-15 minutes.
7. Roll out each dough ball into a thin round shape.
8. Transfer the rolled-out dough onto a baking sheet or pizza stone.
9. Brush the dough with olive oil and add your favorite toppings.
10. Bake the pizzas in the preheated oven for about 10-12 minutes, or until the crust is golden brown and the toppings are cooked.
11. Slice and serve the pizzas hot.

Nutrition Value (per serving): Calories: 290; Proteins: 9g; Carbs: 55g; Fats: 3g; Cholesterol: 0mg; Sodium: 590mg

5. CRACKERS

Prep Time: 15 minutes   **Total Time:** 45 minutes   **Servings:** 6

INGREDIENTS

- 1 cup sourdough discard
- 2 tablespoons olive oil
- 1 teaspoon salt
- 1/2 teaspoon garlic powder
- 1/4 teaspoon paprika
- Optional toppings: sesame seeds, poppy seeds, dried herbs

DIRECTIONS

1. Preheat your oven at 375°F (190°C) and use parchment paper to cover a baking sheet.
2. In a bowl, mix together the sourdough discard, olive oil, salt, garlic powder, and paprika.
3. Roll out the dough on a floured surface until it's about 1/8-inch thick.
4. Cut the dough into desired cracker shapes using a knife or cookie cutter.
5. Place the crackers on the prepared baking sheet and sprinkle with optional toppings if desired.
6. Bake for 15-20 minutes, or until the crackers are golden brown and crispy.
7. Remove them out of your oven let them cool completely before serving.

Nutrition Value (per serving): Calories: 140; Proteins: 3g; Carbs: 20g; Fats: 5g; Cholesterol: 0mg; Sodium: 420mg

6. PRETZELS

Prep Time: 20 minutes   **Total Time:** 1 hour 30 minutes   **Servings:** 8

INGREDIENTS

- 1 1/2 cups sourdough discard
- 3 1/2 cups bread flour
- 1 tablespoon sugar
- 2 teaspoons salt
- 1 cup warm water
- 2 tablespoons baking soda
- Coarse salt for sprinkling
- 1/4 cup melted butter (for brushing)

DIRECTIONS

1. In a huge bowl, combine the sourdough discard, bread flour, sugar, salt, and warm water. Mix until the dough comes together.
2. Transfer the dough to a floured surface and knead for about 5 minutes, or till it becomes smooth and elastic.
3. Place the dough inside a greased dish, cover it using a clean kitchen towel, and let it rise for 1 hour.
4. Preheat your oven at 450°F (230°C) and use parchment paper to cover a baking sheet.
5. Divide the dough into 8 equal portions and roll each portion into a rope about 20 inches long.
6. Shape each rope into a pretzel shape and place them on the prepared baking sheet.
7. In a large pot, bring water to a boil and add the baking soda.
8. Boil each pretzel for 30 seconds on each side, then transfer them back to the baking sheet.
9. Sprinkle the pretzels with coarse salt and bake for 12-15 minutes, or until they turn golden brown.
10. Remove out of your oven brush the pretzels with melted butter.
11. Let them cool slightly before serving.

Nutrition Value (per serving): Calories: 260; Proteins: 8g; Carbs: 50g; Fats: 2g; Cholesterol: 0mg; Sodium: 1870mg

7. BISCUITS

Prep Time: 15 minutes   **Total Time:** 30 minutes   **Servings:** 8

INGREDIENTS

- 2 cups flour
- 2 teaspoons baking powder
- 1/2 teaspoon of salt
- 1/2 cup of cold cubed unsalted butter
- One cup sourdough discard
- 1/2 cup buttermilk
- 1/2 teaspoon of baking soda
- 1 tablespoon honey

DIRECTIONS

1. Preheat your oven at 425°F (220°C) and use parchment paper to cover a baking sheet.
2. In a huge dish, whisk together the salt, baking soda, baking powder, and flour.
3. Add the cold butter to the flour mixture and use a pastry cutter or your fingertips to cut the butter into the flour to the point that the mixture resembles crushed crumbs.
4. In a separate bowl, combine the sourdough discard, buttermilk, and honey. Mix well.
5. Mix wet ingredients and dry ingredients and stir until just combined.
6. To bring the dough together, turn it out onto a floured surface and knead it a few times.
7. Roll the dough to a thickness of about 3/4 inch, then use a round biscuit cutter to cut out biscuits.
8. Place the biscuits onto the prepared baking sheet, leaving a small space between each biscuit.
9. Bake for 12-15 minutes, or until the biscuits are golden brown.
10. Serve the biscuits warm with butter or your favorite toppings.

Nutrition Value (per serving): Calories: 240; Proteins: 4g; Carbs: 31g; Fats: 11g; Cholesterol: 30mg; Sodium: 470mg

8. MUFFINS

Prep Time: 15 minutes   **Total Time:** 35 minutes   **Servings:** 12

INGREDIENTS

- 2 cups of flour
- 1/2 cup milk
- 2 teaspoons of baking powder
- 1/2 teaspoon of baking soda
- 1/2 teaspoon of salt
- 1 cup sourdough discard
- Optional mix-ins: chocolate chips, nuts, berries
- 1/2 cup vegetable oil
- 2 large eggs
- 1/2 cup granulated sugar
- 1 tsp. of vanilla extract

DIRECTIONS

1. Preheat your oven at 375°F (190°C) and line a muffin tin with paper liners.
2. In a huge dish, whisk together the salt, baking soda, sugar, baking powder, and flour.
3. The sourdough scraps, eggs, milk, vegetable oil, and vanilla extract should be mixed together in a separate dish. Toss everything together.
4. Stir together the liquid and dry components till they are just mixed. There may be lumps in the batter.
5. Mix in any extras you like, such berries, chocolate chips, or nuts.
6. Make sure that each muffin tin is about two-thirds full with the batter.
7. Bake for 18-20 minutes, or when a toothpick is put into the center of a muffin arrives clear.
8. Remove out of your oven let the muffins cool in the tin for a few minutes before transferring them to a wire rack to cool completely.

Nutrition Value (per serving): Calories: 230; Proteins: 4g; Carbs: 29g; Fats: 11g; Cholesterol: 30mg; Sodium: 280mg

9. SCONES

Prep Time: 15 minutes   **Total Time:** 30 minutes   **Servings:** 8

INGREDIENTS

- 2 cups flour
- 1/4 cup granulated sugar
- 2 teaspoons baking powder
- 1/2 teaspoon salt
- 1/2 cup of cold cubed unsalted butter
- One cup sourdough discard
- 1/4 cup milk
- 1 tsp. Vanilla extract
- Optional add-ins: dried fruit, chocolate chips, nuts

DIRECTIONS

1. Preheat your oven at 425°F (220°C) and use parchment paper to cover a baking sheet.
2. In a huge dish, whisk together the flour, sugar, baking powder, and salt.
3. Add the cold butter to the flour mixture and use a pastry cutter or your fingertips to cut the butter into the flour to the point that the mixture resembles crushed crumbs.
4. In a separate bowl, combine the sourdough discard, milk, as well as vanilla essence. Mix well.
5. Mix wet ingredients and dry ingredients and stir until just combined.
6. If desired, fold in your chosen add-ins, such as dried fruit, chocolate chips, or nuts.
7. To bring the dough together, turn it out onto a floured surface and knead it a few times.
8. Pat the dough into a circle about 1-inch thick, then cut it into 8 wedges.
9. Place the scones onto the prepared baking sheet, leaving a small space between each scone.
10. Bake for 15-18 minutes, or until the scones are golden brown.
11. Allow the scones to cool slightly before serving.

Nutrition Value (per serving): Calories: 290; Proteins: 4g; Carbs: 34g; Fats: 16g; Cholesterol: 40mg; Sodium: 300mg

10. CHOCOLATE CHIP COOKIES

Prep Time: 15 minutes   **Total Time:** 30 minutes   **Servings:** 24 cookies

INGREDIENTS

- 1/2 cup unsalted butter, softened
- 1/2 cup refined sugar
- 1/2 cup brown sugar
- 1/2 cup sourdough discard
- 2 cups of all-purpose flour,
- 1 large egg,
- 1tsp. vanilla extract,
- 1/2 tsp. baking soda,
- 1/2tsp. salt,
- 1 cup of chocolate chips.

DIRECTIONS

1. Preheat your oven at 375°F (190°C) and use parchment paper to cover a baking sheet.
2. In huge bowl, cream together the softened butter, refined sugar, and brown sugar until light and fluffy.
3. Add the sourdough discard, egg, as well as vanilla essence to the creamed mixture. Mix well.
4. Combine the baking soda, flour, and salt inside a separate bowl.
5. Gradually add the dry ingredients to the wet ingredients, mixing until just combined.
6. Fold in the chocolate chips until evenly distributed throughout the dough.
7. Drop rounded tablespoons of dough placing each piece about 2 inches apart on the prepared baking sheet.
8. Bake for 10-12 minutes, or until the cookies are golden brown around the edges.
9. Remove out of your oven let the cookies cool on the baking sheet for a few minutes before transferring them to a wire rack to cool completely.

Nutrition Value (per serving): Calories: 140; Proteins: 2g; Carbs: 20g; Fats: 6g; Cholesterol: 20mg; Sodium: 80mg

11. BROWNIES

Prep Time: 15 minutes   **Total Time:** 45 minutes   **Servings:** 12

INGREDIENTS

- 1/4 teaspoon of salt
- 1 cup of sourdough discard
- 1/2 cup of melted unsalted butter
- 2 large eggs
- 1/2 cup of all-purpose flour
- 1 teaspoon of vanilla extract
- 1/3 cup of unsweetened cocoa powder
- 1 cup of granulated sugar
- 1/2 cup chocolate chips (optional)

DIRECTIONS

1. Prepare a 9-by-9-inch baking dish by greasing it or lining it with parchment paper and placing it in a preheated 350°F (175°C) oven.
2. Mix the sourdough scraps, sugar, eggs, melted butter, and vanilla extract in a large-sized bowl. Toss everything together.
3. Separately, whisk together the dry ingredients (cocoa powder, flour, and salt).
4. Add the dry components to the wet ones little by little and stir till incorporated.
5. Add the chocolate chips if you'd like.
6. Spread the batter evenly in the prepared baking dish.
7. Cook for 25 to 30 minutes, or until a toothpick inserted in the center emerges out with some moist crumbs attached.
8. Don't cut the brownies till they've cooled completely in the dish.

Nutrition Value (per serving): Calories: 220; Proteins: 3g; Carbs: 29g; Fats: 11g; Cholesterol: 55mg; Sodium: 90mg

12. BAGELS

Prep Time: 30 minutes   **Total Time:** 3 hours   **Servings:** 8 bagels

INGREDIENTS

- 1 cup sourdough discard
- 1 1/2 teaspoons of salt
- 2 tablespoons granulated sugar
- 2 teaspoons active dry yeast
- 1 1/2 cups of warm water
- 4 cups of bread flour
- Optional toppings: sesame seeds, poppy seeds, everything bagel seasoning

DIRECTIONS

1. In a large mixing bowl, combine the sourdough discard, warm water, sugar, and yeast. Let it sit for 5 minutes until the yeast becomes frothy.
2. Add the salt and bread flour to the bowl. Stir until the dough starts to come together.
3. Transfer the dough to a floured surface and knead for about 10 minutes until elastic and smooth.
4. Place the dough inside a greased dish, cover using a kitchen towel, then let it proof for two to three hours in a warm spot, or until size has more than doubled.
5. Punch down the dough and divide it into eight equal-sized portions.
6. Shape each portion into a ball, then poke a hole in the center with your thumb.
7. Gently stretch the hole to form a bagel shape.
8. Put the shaped bagels on a parchment-lined baking tray and let them rest for 15-20 minutes.
9. Meanwhile, warm your oven at 425°F (220°C) and get a large-sized pot of water to boil.
10. Boil the bagels, a few at a time, for 1-2 minutes on each side. Remove them from the water and put them back on the baking tray.
11. If desired, sprinkle the bagels with your choice of toppings.
12. Bake the bagels for 20-25 minutes, or until they are golden brown.
13. Let the bagels cool on a wire rack before slicing and serving.

Nutrition Value (per serving): Calories: 260; Proteins: 9g; Carbs: 54g; Fats: 1g; Cholesterol: 0mg; Sodium: 390mg

13. CINNAMON ROLLS

Prep Time: 30 minutes   **Total Time:** 2 hours 30 minutes   **Servings:** 12

INGREDIENTS

For the dough:
- 1 cup sourdough discard
- 1/2 cup milk
- 1/4 cup unsalted butter, melted
- 1/4 cup granulated sugar
- 1 teaspoon salt
- 3 1/2 cups all-purpose flour
- 2 teaspoons instant yeast
- 1 large egg

For the filling:
- 1/4 cup unsalted butter, softened
- 1/2 cup brown sugar
- 2 teaspoons ground cinnamon

For the glaze:
- 1 cup powdered sugar
- 2 tablespoons milk
- 1/2 teaspoon vanilla extract

DIRECTIONS

1. Inside a small saucepan, heat the milk until it is warm but not boiling. Remove from heat.
2. In a huge bowl, combine the sourdough discard, melted butter, sugar, and salt. Stir until well combined.
3. Add the warm milk to the sourdough mixture and stir to combine.
4. In a separate bowl, combine the flour and instant yeast.
5. Gradually add the flour mixture to the sourdough mixture, stirring until a soft dough forms.
6. Turn the dough out onto a board that has been lightly dusted with flour and knead for about 5 minutes, or until the dough is elastic and smooth.
7. Place the dough inside a greased dish, cover using a clean kitchen towel, then let it proof for two to three hours in a warm spot, or until size has more than doubled.
8. On a lightly floured board, punch down the dough and roll it out into a broad rectangle.
9. Lay out the softened butter equally over the dough.
10. Inside a small bowl, combine the ground cinnamon and brown sugar. Sprinkle the combination over the buttered dough.
11. Starting from one of the long edges, roll dough tightly into a log.
12. Using a sharp knife or dental floss, cut the log into 12 equal-sized rolls.
13. Place the rolls in a greased baking dish, leaving a small space between each roll.
14. Cover the dish with a kitchen towel and let the rolls rise for an additional 30 minutes.
15. Preheat your oven to 375°F (190°C).
16. Bake the cinnamon rolls for 20-25 minutes, or until they are golden light brown.
17. While the rolls are baking, prepare the glaze by whisking together the powdered sugar, milk, as well as vanilla essence in a small bowl until smooth.
18. Remove the rolls out of your oven let them cool for a few minutes.
19. Drizzle the glaze over the warm cinnamon rolls & serve.

Nutrition Value (per serving): Calories: 280; Proteins: 5g; Carbs: 50g; Fats: 7g; Cholesterol: 35mg; Sodium: 230mg

14. ENGLISH MUFFINS

Prep Time: 20 minutes   **Total Time:** 1 hour 30 minutes   **Servings:** 8 muffins

INGREDIENTS

- 1 cup sourdough discard
- 1/2 cup milk
- 2 tablespoons unsalted butter, melted
- 2 tablespoons granulated sugar
- 3 cups all-purpose flour
- 1 teaspoon salt
- 1 teaspoon baking soda
- Cornmeal, for dusting

DIRECTIONS

1. In a large mixing bowl, combine the sourdough discard, milk, melted butter, and sugar. Mix well.
2. In a separate dish, whisk together the flour, salt, and baking soda.
3. Gradually add the dry ingredients to the sourdough mixture, stirring until a soft dough forms.
4. Turn the dough out onto a floured surface and knead for about 5 minutes until elastic and smooth.
5. Roll out the dough to a thickness of about 1/2 inch. Using a round cookie cutter or a drinking glass, cut out circles from the dough.
6. Place the muffins on a baking sheet dusted with cornmeal. Cover with a clean kitchen towel and let them rise for 30 minutes.
7. Preheat a skillet or griddle over medium heat.
8. Cook the muffins for about 5 minutes on each side, or until golden brown and cooked through.
9. Remove the muffins from the skillet and let them cool on a wire rack before splitting and toasting.

Nutrition Value (per serving): Calories: 190; Proteins: 5g; Carbs: 37g; Fats: 2g; Cholesterol: 5mg; Sodium: 400mg

15. TORTILLAS

Prep Time: 15 minutes   **Total Time:** 30 minutes   **Servings:** Makes 10 tortillas

INGREDIENTS

- 1 cup sourdough discard
- 2 cups all-purpose flour
- 1/2 teaspoon salt
- 2 tablespoons vegetable oil
- 1/2 cup warm water

DIRECTIONS

1. In a huge bowl, combine the sourdough discard, flour, salt, and vegetable oil. Mix well.
2. Gradually add the warm water to the mixture, stirring until a soft dough forms.
3. Turn the dough out onto a board that has been lightly dusted with flour and knead for a few minutes until smooth.
4. Divide the dough into 10 equal-sized portions and shape each portion into a ball.
5. Cover the dough balls with a clean kitchen towel and let them rest for 10 minutes.
6. Preheat a skillet or griddle over medium heat.
7. Roll out each dough ball into a thin, round tortilla.
8. Cook each tortilla on the preheated skillet for about 1 minute on each side, or until lightly browned and cooked through.
9. Repeat with the remaining dough balls.
10. Serve the tortillas warm and use them for your favorite dishes.

Nutrition Value (per serving - 1 tortilla): Calories: 120; Proteins: 3g; Carbs: 20g; Fats: 3g; Cholesterol: 0mg; Sodium: 120mg

16. FOCACCIA BREAD

Prep Time: 15 minutes   **Total Time:** 2 hours 15 minutes   **Servings:** Makes 1 loaf

INGREDIENTS

- 1 cup sourdough discard
- 2 1/2 cups bread flour
- 1 teaspoon salt
- 1/2 teaspoon dried rosemary
- 1/2 teaspoon dried thyme
- 1/4 cup olive oil
- 1/2 cup warm water

DIRECTIONS

1. In a huge bowl, combine the sourdough discard, bread flour, salt, dried rosemary, dried thyme, olive oil, and warm water. Mix well.
2. The dough should be kneaded on a surface that is lightly floured for about 5 minutes, or until it is smooth and elastic.
3. Place the dough inside a greased dish, cover using a clean kitchen towel, then let it proof for two to three hours in a warm spot, or until size has more than doubled.
4. Preheat your oven to 425°F (220°C) and grease a baking sheet or line it with parchment paper.
5. Punch down the dough and transfer it to the prepared baking sheet. Press it down gently to form a rectangle or square shape.
6. Drizzle the top of the dough with olive oil and use your fingertips to make dimples all over the surface.
7. Sprinkle additional dried rosemary and thyme over the top, if desired.
8. Bake the focaccia bread in the preheated oven for 20-25 minutes, or until golden brown.
9. Remove out of your oven let it cool on a wire rack before slicing and serving.

Nutrition Value (per serving): Calories: 180; Proteins: 5g; Carbs: 30g; Fats: 5g; Cholesterol: 0mg; Sodium: 200mg

17. FLATBREAD

Prep Time: 15 minutes   **Total Time:** 30 minutes   **Servings:** Makes 4-6 flatbreads

INGREDIENTS

- 1 cup sourdough discard
- 2 cups all-purpose flour
- 1/2 teaspoon salt
- 2 tablespoons olive oil
- 1/2 cup warm water

DIRECTIONS

1. In a huge bowl, combine the sourdough discard, flour, salt, olive oil, and warm water. Mix well.
2. Gradually add the warm water to the mixture, stirring until a soft dough forms.
3. Turn the dough out onto a board that has been lightly dusted with flour and knead for a few minutes until smooth.
4. Divide the dough into 4-6 equal-sized portions and shape each portion into a ball.
5. Cover the dough balls with a clean kitchen towel and let them rest for 10 minutes.
6. Preheat a skillet or griddle over medium heat.
7. Roll out each dough ball into a thin, round flatbread.
8. Cook each flatbread on the preheated skillet for about 2-3 minutes on each side, or until lightly browned and cooked through.
9. Repeat with the remaining dough balls.
10. Serve the flatbreads warm and use them as a base for wraps, sandwiches, or as a side to your favorite dishes.

Nutrition Value (per serving - 1 flatbread): Calories: 180; Proteins: 5g; Carbs: 30g; Fats: 4g; Cholesterol: 0mg; Sodium: 200mg

18. DOUGHNUTS

Prep Time: 30 minutes   **Total Time:** 2 hours 30 minutes   **Servings:** Makes 12 doughnuts

INGREDIENTS

- **For the doughnuts:**
- 1 cup sourdough discard
- 1/2 cup milk
- 2 teaspoons of baking powder
- Vegetable oil, for frying
- 4 cups flour
- 1/4 cup granulated sugar
- 2 large eggs
- 1 teaspoon vanilla extract
- 1/2 teaspoon of baking soda
- 4 tablespoons unsalted butter, melted
- 1/2 teaspoon salt
- **For the glaze:**
- 1/4 cup milk
- 1 teaspoon of vanilla extract
- 2 cups powdered sugar

DIRECTIONS

1. Inside a large-sized mixing bowl, combine the milk, sourdough discard, sugar, melted butter, eggs, as well as vanilla essence. Mix well.
2. In a separate dish, whisk together the baking soda, flour, baking powder, and salt.
3. To make a soft dough, add the dry components to the sourdough combination gradually while stirring.
4. Turn the dough out onto a floured surface and knead for about 5 minutes until elastic and smooth.
5. Place the dough inside a greased dish, cover using a clean kitchen towel, then let it proof for two to three hours in a warm spot, or until size has more than doubled.
6. Punch down the dough and roll it out to a thickness of about 1/2 inch.
7. Use a doughnut cutter or two round cookie cutters to cut out doughnut shapes.
8. Place the doughnuts on a baking sheet lined with parchment paper and let them rest for 20-30 minutes.
9. Meanwhile, heat vegetable oil in a deep pot or deep fryer to 350°F (175°C).
10. Carefully add a few doughnuts to the hot oil and fry for 2-3 minutes on each side, or until golden brown.
11. Remove the doughnuts from the oil and drain them on a paper towel-lined plate.
12. Repeat with the remaining doughnuts.
13. In a small dish, whisk together the powdered sugar, milk, as well as vanilla essence to make the glaze.
14. Dip each doughnut into the glaze, allowing the excess to drip off.
15. Place the glazed doughnuts on a wire rack to set.
16. Serve the doughnuts fresh and enjoy!

Nutrition Value (per serving - 1 doughnut): Calories: 250; Proteins: 4g; Carbs: 47g; Fats: 6g; Cholesterol: 35mg; Sodium: 200mg

19. CAKES

Prep Time: 20 minutes   **Total Time:** 1 hour 30 minutes   **Servings:** Varies based on cake size

INGREDIENTS

- 1 cup of sourdough discard
- 1 cup of flour
- 1/2 cup milk
- 1/2 teaspoon of baking soda
- 1/2 teaspoon salt
- 1 cup granulated sugar
- 1/2 cup of unsalted softened butter
- 1/2 teaspoon of baking powder
- 2 large eggs
- 1 teaspoon vanilla extract

DIRECTIONS

1. Preheat your oven at 350°F (175°C). Grease and flour a cake pan.
2. Mix the sourdough scraps, baking soda, flour, baking powder, with salt into a medium bowl.
3. Softened butter and sugar are mixed till frothy within a separate large-sized mixing dish.
4. Beat in the eggs one at a time, followed by the vanilla extract.
5. The dry components should be added to the butter combination in three additions, followed by the milk. Combine to avoid clumping.
6. Spread the batter evenly over the bottom of the prepared cake pan. Bake in the preheated oven for 25-30 minutes, or when a toothpick is put into the middle arrives clear.
7. Remove the cake out of your oven let it cool in the pan for 10 minutes. Then transfer it to a wire rack to cool completely.
8. Once the cake is cool, you can frost it with your favorite frosting or enjoy it as is.

Nutrition Value: Calories: 2640; Fat: 108g; Carbohydrates: 386g; Protein: 42g; Cholesterol: 460mg; Sodium: 2270mg

20. PITA BREAD

Prep Time: 20 minutes   **Total Time:** 2 hours   **Servings:** Makes 8 pita breads

INGREDIENTS

- 1 cup sourdough discard
- 2 cups all-purpose flour
- 1 teaspoon salt
- 1 teaspoon sugar
- 1 teaspoon active dry yeast
- 1 tablespoon olive oil
- 3/4 cup warm water

DIRECTIONS

1. Inside a large-sized mixing dish, combine the flour, sourdough discard, salt, sugar, yeast, olive oil, and warm water. Mix well.
2. Knead the dough for about 5-7 minutes till it becomes smooth and elastic.
3. Place the dough inside a greased dish, cover with a clean kitchen towel, then let it proof for two to three hours in a warm spot, or until size has more than doubled.
4. Preheat your oven to 500°F (260°C) with a baking stone or baking sheet inside.
5. Punch down the dough and divide it into eight equal-sized portions. Shape each portion into a ball.
6. Each ball should be rolled out into a thin circle, 6-8 inches in diameter, on a surface that is lightly floured.
7. Carefully transfer the rolled-out dough to the preheated baking stone or baking sheet.
8. Bake the pita breads for 5-6 minutes, or until puffed up and lightly browned.
9. Remove them out of your oven let them cool over a wire rack.
10. Serve the pita breads warm or at room temperature, and use them for sandwiches, wraps, or as a side to dips and spreads.

Nutrition Value (per serving - 1 pita bread): Calories: 150; Proteins: 4g; Carbs: 28g; Fats: 2g; Cholesterol: 0mg; Sodium: 200mg

21. GARLIC KNOTS

Prep Time: 15 minutes   **Total Time:** 1 hour 15 minutes   **Servings:** Makes 12 garlic knots

INGREDIENTS

- 1 cup sourdough discard
- 2 1/2 cups all-purpose flour
- 2 teaspoons sugar
- 1 teaspoon salt
- 2 teaspoons active dry yeast
- 1/2 cup warm water
- 2 tablespoons olive oil
- 3 cloves garlic, minced
- 2 tablespoons unsalted butter, melted
- 1 tablespoon chopped fresh parsley (optional)
- Salt, for sprinkling

DIRECTIONS

1. In a small bowl, dissolve the yeast and sugar in warm water. Let it sit for 5 minutes, or until foamy.
2. Inside a large-sized mixing dish, combine the flour, sourdough discard, salt, and olive oil. Mix well.
3. Add the yeast mixture to the bowl and mix until a soft dough forms.
4. Turn the dough out onto a floured surface and knead for about 5 minutes until elastic and smooth.
5. Place the dough inside a greased dish, cover with a clean kitchen towel, and let it rise in a warm place for 1 hour, or until size has more than doubled.
6. Turn the oven on to 375 degrees Fahrenheit (190 degrees Celsius). Use parchment paper to line a baking sheet.
7. Punch down the dough and divide it into 12 equal-sized portions. Roll each portion into a rope and tie it into a knot.
8. Place the garlic knots on the prepared baking sheet, spacing them apart.
9. In a small bowl, combine the minced garlic and melted butter.
10. Brush the garlic butter mixture over the knots, ensuring they are well coated.
11. Sprinkle the knots with salt and chopped fresh parsley, if desired.
12. Bake in the preheated oven for 15-20 minutes, or until golden brown.
13. Remove them out of your oven let them cool slightly before serving.

Nutrition Value (per serving - 1 garlic knot): Calories: 150; Proteins: 4g; Carbs: 25g; Fats: 3g; Cholesterol: 5mg; Sodium: 200mg

22. PANCAKES

Prep Time: 10 minutes   **Total Time:** 25 minutes   **Servings:** Makes 10-12 pancakes

INGREDIENTS

- 1 cup sourdough discard
- 1 large egg
- 1 cup flour
- 1/2 teaspoon salt
- 1 teaspoon of vanilla extract
- 2 tablespoons of sugar
- 1 cup milk
- 1/2 teaspoon of baking soda
- 2 tablespoons unsalted butter, melted
- 1 teaspoon of baking powder

DIRECTIONS

1. Inside a large-sized mixing dish, combine the flour, baking soda, sourdough discard, salt, baking powder, and sugar. Mix well.
2. In a separate dish, whisk together the milk, egg, melted butter, as well as vanilla essence.
3. Combine the dry and wet components by pouring the wet into the dry and stirring together. The batter should have some lumps; over mixing will make them disappear.
4. Let the batter rest for 10 minutes to allow the sourdough discard to activate and the flavors to meld.
5. Preheat a griddle or non-stick skillet with moderate heat. Lightly grease with butter or cooking spray.
6. Spread a quarter cup of batter per pancake on the griddle. When bubbles begin to appear on the surface, flip the food and cook for a further minute, till it is golden brown.
7. Use the remaining batter in the same manner.
8. Serve pancakes warm with your favorite toppings such as maple syrup, fresh fruits, or whipped cream.

Nutrition Value (per serving - 1 pancake): Calories: 120; Proteins: 4g; Carbs: 19g; Fats: 3g; Cholesterol: 25mg; Sodium: 200mg

23. BANANA NUTMEG BREAD

Prep Time: 15 minutes   **Total Time:** 1 hour 15 minutes   **Servings:** 1 loaf

INGREDIENTS

- 1/4 teaspoon ground nutmeg
- 1 cup sourdough discard
- 1/2 teaspoon salt
- 3 ripe bananas, mashed
- 1/2 cup unsalted melted butter
- 1 teaspoon vanilla extract
- 2 large eggs
- 1/2 teaspoon ground cinnamon
- 1 teaspoon of baking soda
- 3/4 cup brown sugar
- 1/2 cup chopped nuts (optional)
- 1 1/2 cups of all-purpose flour

DIRECTIONS

1. Preheat your oven at 350°F (175°C). Grease a 9x5-inch loaf pan.
2. Inside a large-sized mixing dish, combine the flour, cinnamon, sourdough discard, salt, baking soda, and nutmeg. Mix well.
3. Whisk the brown sugar into the melted butter in a separate dish.
4. Gradually include the eggs, mixing thoroughly after each addition. Blend in some vanilla essence.
5. The mashed bananas should be added to the wet components and thoroughly combined.
6. Mix both the wet and dry components by slowly adding the wet ingredients to the dry ones. Avoid blending too much.
7. If using chopped nuts, add them in now.
8. After preheating the loaf pan, pour the mixture into it and smooth the top using a spatula.
9. Bake for 50-60 minutes in a preheated oven, or till a toothpick inserted in the middle comes out clean.
10. After 10 minutes, take the banana bread out of the oven and allow it cool in the pan. Then, put it on a cooling rack to cool to room temperature.
11. Banana bread can be served in whatever slices you like.

Nutrition Value (per serving - 1 slice): Calories: 220; Proteins: 4g; Carbs: 32g; Fats: 9g; Cholesterol: 55mg; Sodium: 250mg

24. PIZZA DISCARD

Prep Time: 15 minutes

Total Time: 1 hour 30 minutes

Servings: Makes 2 medium-sized pizzas

INGREDIENTS

- 1 cup sourdough discard
- 2 1/2 cups all-purpose flour
- 1 teaspoon salt
- 1 teaspoon sugar
- 1 teaspoon active dry yeast
- 1 tablespoon olive oil
- 3/4 cup warm water

DIRECTIONS

1. Sugar and yeast should be dissolved in warm water in a small-sized bowl. Give it 5 minutes to froth up.
2. Flour, salt, sourdough scraps, and olive oil should all be mixed together in a big bowl. Toss everything together.
3. The yeast mixture should be added to the bowl and the dough should be soft after being mixed.
4. To get an elastic and smooth dough, turn it out onto an area of flour and knead for approximately five minutes.
5. After the dough has doubled in size, place it in an oiled dish, cover with a clean towel from the kitchen, and set it in a warm area.
6. Turn on your oven's highest heat setting (typically between 475 and 500 degrees Fahrenheit, or 245 and 260 degrees Celsius).
7. The dough should be punched down and cut in two. Roll each piece into a ball.
8. On a floured board, roll out each ball of dough to the appropriate thickness.
9. Placing the dough on a pizza stone or baking sheet is the next step after rolling it out.
10. Put on some tomato paste, some cheese, some veggies, and some meat if you like.
11. Preheat the oven to 400 degrees and bake the pizzas for 10 to 15 minutes, or till the dough is golden and the cheese has become melted and bubbling.
12. Take the pizzas out of the oven and let them cool for a few minutes before cutting them up.

Nutrition Value (per serving - 1 slice): Calories: 180; Proteins: 4g; Carbs: 34g; Fats: 2g; Cholesterol: 0mg; Sodium: 300mg

CHAPTER 13
QUICK BREADS AND PANCAKES

1. BANANA BREAD

Prep Time: 15 minutes   **Total Time:** 1 hour 15 minutes   **Servings:** 10 slices

INGREDIENTS

- 1/2 teaspoon of salt
- 1 cup of sourdough starter
- 1/2 cup of unsalted butter, melted
- 1 3/4 cups of all-purpose flour
- 1 cup of granulated sugar
- 1 teaspoon of baking soda
- 2 eggs
- 1 teaspoon of vanilla extract
- 2 ripe mashed bananas

DIRECTIONS

1. Preheat the oven at 350°F (175°C). Grease a nine by five-inch loaf pan.
2. In a large-sized dish, combine the sourdough starter, mashed bananas, melted butter, sugar, eggs, as well as vanilla essence.
3. Combine the flour, baking soda, and salt inside a separate bowl. Mix the dry components into the wet ones till everything is evenly distributed.
4. Then, pour the mixture into the pan and level the top.
5. Bake for around 50 to 60 minutes, or till a toothpick inserted in the middle of the cake pulls out clean.
6. After ten minutes, remove the banana bread from the pan to a wire rack for cooling fully.

Nutrition Value (per slice): Calories: 240; Protein: 4g; Carbs: 38g; Fat: 8g; Cholesterol: 50mg; Sodium: 220mg

2. LEMON POPPY SEED SOURDOUGH BREAD

Prep Time: 20 minutes   **Total Time:** 3 hours   **Servings:** 12 slices

INGREDIENTS

- 1 cup sourdough starter
- 1/2 cup milk
- 1/4 cup lemon juice
- Zest of 1 lemon
- 1/2 cup unsalted butter, melted
- 1 cup granulated sugar
- 2 eggs
- 1/2 teaspoon of baking soda
- 2 cups flour
- 1 tablespoon poppy seeds
- 1 teaspoon of baking powder
- 1/2 teaspoon salt

DIRECTIONS

1. The sourdough starter, sugar, milk, lemon juice, melted butter, lemon zest, and eggs should all be combined in a large basin.
2. To make the batter, combine the flour, baking soda, poppy seeds, baking powder, and salt in a separate bowl and whisk till smooth.
3. Add the dry components to the liquid and whisk till incorporated.
4. Put the mixture into a buttered 9x5-inch bread pan.
5. Bake at 350 degrees Fahrenheit (175 degrees Celsius) for 50 to 60 minutes, or till a toothpick placed in the middle comes out clear.
6. After ten minutes, remove the bread from the pan and place it on a wire rack for cooling entirely.

Nutrition Value (per slice): Calories: 250; Protein: 4g; Carbs: 38g; Fat: 9g; Cholesterol: 50mg; Sodium: 240mg

3. BLUEBERRY MUFFINS

Prep Time: 15 minutes   **Total Time:** 35 minutes   **Servings:** 12 muffins

INGREDIENTS

- 1 1/2 cups of fresh or frozen blueberries
- 1 cup sourdough starter
- 1/2 cup of milk
- 1 1/2 teaspoons of baking powder
- 1/4 cup of vegetable oil
- 2 eggs
- 1/2 teaspoon of salt
- 1 teaspoon of vanilla extract
- 1/2 cup of granulated sugar
- 2 cups of flour
- 1/2 teaspoon of baking soda

DIRECTIONS

1. Turn the oven temperature up to 375 degrees Fahrenheit (190 degrees Celsius). Use paper liners or oil a muffin tray.
2. Inside a large-sized bowl, mix together the eggs, sourdough starter, vegetable oil, milk, sugar, as well as vanilla essence.
3. In a separate dish, whisk together the baking soda, flour, baking powder, and salt.
4. Add the dry components to the liquid and whisk till incorporated.
5. Mix the blueberries in gently.
6. Divide the batter evenly among the muffin cups, filling each about 2/3 full.
7. Bake for 18-20 minutes, or when a toothpick is put into the center arrives clear.
8. Remove the muffins from the tin and let them cool on a wire rack.

Nutrition Value (per muffin): Calories: 180; Protein: 4g; Carbs: 29g; Fat: 6g; Cholesterol: 30mg; Sodium: 220mg

4. CINNAMON SWIRL SOURDOUGH BREAD

Prep Time: 30 minutes   **Total Time:** 4 hours   **Servings:** 12 slices

INGREDIENTS

- 1 cup sourdough starter
- 1/2 cup milk
- 1/4 cup unsalted butter, melted
- 1/4 cup granulated sugar
- 1 teaspoon vanilla extract
- 2 cups flour
- 1 teaspoon of baking powder
- 1/2 teaspoon salt
- 1/4 cup granulated sugar
- 1 tablespoon ground cinnamon
- 1/2 teaspoon of baking soda

DIRECTIONS

1. In a huge bowl, combine the sourdough starter, milk, melted butter, sugar, as well as vanilla essence.
2. In a separate dish, whisk together the flour, baking powder, baking soda, and salt.
3. Add the dry components to the wet and whisk till incorporated.
4. To make the swirl filling, combine sugar and cinnamon in a small-sized dish.
5. Divide the batter in half and grease a 9-by-5-inch loaf pan. Divide the cinnamon sugar blend in half and sprinkle half of it over the batter.
6. Pour the remaining batter on top and sprinkle the remaining cinnamon sugar mixture over it. Use a knife to gently swirl the batter and cinnamon sugar.
7. Let the bread rise in a warm place for 2-3 hours, or until size has more than doubled.
8. Preheat the oven to 350°F (175°C). Bake the bread for 40-50 minutes, or until golden brown and a toothpick inserted into the center arrives clear.
9. Allow the bread to cool in the pan for 10 minutes, then transfer it to a wire rack to cool completely.

Nutrition Value (per slice): Calories: 200; Protein: 3g; Carbs: 36g; Fat: 5g; Cholesterol: 15mg; Sodium: 220mg

5. PUMPKIN PANCAKES

Prep Time: 10 minutes   **Total Time:** 25 minutes   **Servings:** 4

INGREDIENTS

- 1 cup sourdough starter
- 1/2 cup canned pumpkin puree
- 2 tablespoons granulated sugar
- 1/2 teaspoon ground cinnamon
- 1/4 teaspoon ground nutmeg
- 1/4 teaspoon ground ginger
- 1/4 teaspoon salt
- 1/2 teaspoon baking soda
- 1 egg
- 2 tablespoons melted butter or vegetable oil
- 1/2 cup milk

DIRECTIONS

1. Inside a large-sized bowl, combine the sourdough starter, pumpkin puree, sugar, cinnamon, nutmeg, ginger, salt, baking soda, egg, melted butter or oil, and milk. Mix until well combined.
2. Preheat a griddle or skillet with moderate heat and lightly grease it.
3. Pour about 1/4 cup of the batter onto the grill for each pancake. Cook until small bubbles form on the surface, then flip and cook until golden brown on the other side.
4. Repeat with the remaining batter.
5. Serve the pancakes warm with your favorite toppings such as maple syrup, whipped cream, or chopped nuts.

Nutrition Value (per serving): Calories: 220; Protein: 7g; Carbs: 34g; Fat: 7g; Cholesterol: 55mg; Sodium: 410mg

6. APPLE CIDER SOURDOUGH BREAD

Prep Time: 20 minutes   **Total Time:** 3 hours 30 minutes   **Servings:** 10 slices

INGREDIENTS

- 1 cup sourdough starter
- 1 cup apple cider
- 1/2 teaspoon of baking soda
- 1/4 cup unsalted butter, melted
- 1/4 cup granulated sugar
- 2 cups flour
- 1 teaspoon of baking powder
- 1/2 teaspoon salt
- 1 teaspoon ground cinnamon
- 1/4 teaspoon ground nutmeg
- 1/4 teaspoon ground cloves
- 1/2 cup chopped apples

DIRECTIONS

1. Inside a large-sized bowl, combine the sourdough starter, apple cider, melted butter, and sugar.
2. In a separate dish, whisk together the flour, baking powder, baking soda, salt, cinnamon, nutmeg, and cloves.
3. Gradually add dry components to the wet and whisk till incorporated.
4. Fold in the chopped apples.
5. Pour the batter into a greased 9x5-inch loaf pan.
6. Let the bread rise in a warm place for 2-3 hours, or until size has more than doubled.
7. Preheat the oven to 350°F (175°C). Bake the bread for 50-60 minutes, or when a toothpick is put into the center arrives clear.
8. Allow the bread to cool in the pan for 10 minutes, then transfer it to a wire rack to cool completely.

Nutrition Value (per slice): Calories: 200; Protein: 4g; Carbs: 35g; Fat: 5g; Cholesterol: 15mg; Sodium: 280mg

7. CHOCOLATE CHIP MUFFINS

Prep Time: 15 minutes   **Total Time:** 35 minutes   **Servings:** 12 muffins

INGREDIENTS

- 1 cup sourdough starter
- 1/2 cup milk
- 1/4 cup vegetable oil
- 1/2 cup granulated sugar
- 2 eggs
- 1 teaspoon vanilla extract
- 2 cups flour
- 1 1/2 teaspoons baking powder
- 1/2 teaspoon baking soda
- 1/4 teaspoon salt
- 1 cup chocolate chips

DIRECTIONS

1. Turn the oven temperature up to 375 degrees Fahrenheit (190 degrees Celsius). Use paper liners or oil a muffin tray.
2. Inside a large-sized bowl, mix together the sourdough starter, milk, vegetable oil, sugar, eggs, as well as vanilla essence.
3. In a separate dish, whisk together the flour, baking powder, baking soda, and salt.
4. Gradually add dry components to the wet and whisk till incorporated.
5. Melt the chocolate and mix it in.
6. Divide the batter evenly among the muffin cups, filling each about 2/3 full.
7. Bake for 18-20 minutes, or when a toothpick is put into the center arrives clear.
8. Remove the muffins from the tin and let them cool on a wire rack.

Nutrition Value (per muffin): Calories: 240; Protein: 4g; Carbs: 36g; Fat: 9g; Cholesterol: 30mg; Sodium: 220mg

8. ZUCCHINI BREAD

Prep Time: 15 minutes   **Total Time:** 1 hour 15 minutes   **Servings:** 12 slices

INGREDIENTS

- 1 cup of sourdough starter
- 1 1/2 cups of grated zucchini
- 1/2 cup of vegetable oil
- 1/2 cup of brown sugar
- 1/2 teaspoon of baking soda
- 1 3/4 cups of flour
- 1 teaspoon of vanilla extract
- 1/2 cup of granulated sugar
- 1 teaspoon of baking powder
- 1/2 teaspoon of salt
- 1 teaspoon of ground cinnamon
- 1/2 teaspoon of ground nutmeg
- 2 eggs
- 1/2 cup of chopped walnuts (optional)

DIRECTIONS

1. Set the temperature to 175 degrees Celsius (or 350 degrees Fahrenheit). Prepare a nine by five-inch loaf pan with butter.
2. Combine the sourdough starter, oil, sugars (white and brown), eggs, and vanilla inside a large dish.
3. Add the grated zucchini and mix it in.
4. Flour, cinnamon, baking powder, salt, baking soda, and nutmeg should be mixed together in a separate bowl.
5. Add the dry stuff to wet and stir until combined.
6. If using walnuts, crumble them up and mix them in.
7. Then, pour the mixture into the pan and level the top.
8. Cook for around 50-60 minutes, or until a toothpick placed in the center pulls out clear.
9. After 10 minutes, remove the zucchini bread from the pan to a wire rack for cooling fully.

Nutrition Value (per slice): Calories: 250; Protein: 4g; Carbs: 35g; Fat: 11g; Cholesterol: 30mg; Sodium: 200mg

9. CRANBERRY ORANGE SOURDOUGH PANCAKES

Prep Time: 10 minutes   **Total Time:** 25 minutes   **Servings:** 4

INGREDIENTS

- 1 cup sourdough starter
- 1/2 cup milk
- 2 tablespoons melted butter
- 2 tablespoons orange juice
- Zest of 1 orange
- 2 tablespoons granulated sugar
- 1/2 teaspoon of baking soda
- 1 egg
- 1 cup flour
- 1 teaspoon of baking powder
- 1/4 teaspoon salt
- 1/2 cup fresh or frozen cranberries, chopped

DIRECTIONS

1. The sourdough starter, sugar, milk, orange juice, melted butter, orange zest, and egg should all be mixed together in a big bowl.
2. Flour, baking powder, salt and baking soda should be mixed separately.
3. Add the dry stuff to wet and stir till combined.
4. Add the diced cranberries and mix well.
5. Lightly coat a griddle or pan with oil and heat it over a medium-high flame.
6. For each pancake, use roughly a quarter cup of the batter. Wait for bubbles to form on the outermost layer, flip, and brown the other side.
7. Use the remaining batter in the same manner.
8. Warm the pancakes and serve with maple syrup and toppings of your choice.

Nutrition Value (per serving): Calories: 280; Protein: 6g; Carbs: 45g; Fat: 9g; Cholesterol: 60mg; Sodium: 400mg

10. BANANA BREAD

Prep Time: 15 minutes   **Total Time:** 1 hour 15 minutes   **Servings:** 10 slices

INGREDIENTS

- 1 cup sourdough starter
- 1/2 cup unsalted butter, melted
- 1/2 cup brown sugar
- 1/2 teaspoon of ground cinnamon
- 2 eggs
- 1/2 teaspoon of baking soda
- 1/2 cup of walnuts chopped (optional)
- 1 teaspoon vanilla extract
- 1/2 cup granulated sugar
- 3 ripe bananas, mashed
- 1 3/4 cups flour
- 1 teaspoon of baking powder
- 1/2 teaspoon of salt
- 1/4 teaspoon ground nutmeg

DIRECTIONS

1. Preheat the oven at 350°F (175°C). Grease a nine by five-inch loaf pan.
2. Inside a large-sized bowl, mix together the sourdough starter, melted butter, granulated sugar, brown sugar, eggs, as well as vanilla essence.
3. Stir in the mashed bananas.
4. Inside a separate dish, whisk together the baking soda, flour, cinnamon, baking powder, salt, and nutmeg.
5. Gradually add dry components to the wet and whisk till incorporated.
6. Fold in the chopped walnuts, if using.
7. Pour the batter into the prepared loaf pan and smooth the top.
8. Bake for 50-60 minutes, or when a toothpick is put into the center arrives clear.
9. Allow the banana bread to cool in the pan for 10 minutes, then transfer it to a wire rack to cool completely.

Nutrition Value (per slice): Calories: 290; Protein: 5g; Carbs: 40g; Fat: 13g; Cholesterol: 55mg; Sodium: 250mg

11. BLUEBERRY PANCAKES

Prep Time: 10 minutes   **Total Time:** 25 minutes   **Servings:** 4

INGREDIENTS

- 1 cup sourdough starter
- 1/2 cup milk
- 2 tablespoons melted butter
- 2 tablespoons granulated sugar
- 1 egg
- 1/2 teaspoon of baking soda
- 1 cup flour
- 1 teaspoon of baking powder
- 1/4 teaspoon salt
- 1/2 cup fresh or frozen blueberries

DIRECTIONS

1. Inside a large-sized bowl, combine the sourdough starter, milk, melted butter, sugar, and egg.
2. In a separate dish, whisk together the baking soda, flour, baking powder, and salt.
3. Gradually add dry components to the wet and whisk till incorporated.
4. Fold in the blueberries.
5. Preheat a griddle or skillet with moderate heat and lightly grease it.
6. Pour about 1/4 cup of the batter onto the grill for each pancake. Cook until small bubbles form on the surface, then flip and cook until golden brown on the other side.
7. Repeat with the remaining batter.
8. Serve the pancakes warm with maple syrup or your desired toppings.

Nutrition Value (per serving): Calories: 260; Protein: 6g; Carbs: 42g; Fat: 7g; Cholesterol: 60mg; Sodium: 400mg

12. CINNAMON ROLL PANCAKES

Prep Time: 15 minutes   **Total Time:** 40 minutes   **Serving:** 4

INGREDIENTS

- 1 cup sourdough starter
- 1 cup flour
- 1/2 teaspoon of baking soda
- 1 tablespoon sugar
- 1 teaspoon of baking powder
- 1/2 teaspoon salt
- 1 cup buttermilk
- 1 egg
- 2 tablespoons melted butter
- 1 teaspoon vanilla extract
- **For the cinnamon swirl:**
- 1/4 cup unsalted butter, melted
- 1/4 cup brown sugar
- 1 tablespoon ground cinnamon
- **For the cream cheese glaze:**
- 4 ounces cream cheese, softened
- 1/4 cup powdered sugar
- 2-3 tablespoons milk

DIRECTIONS

1. In a huge bowl, combine the sourdough starter, salt, baking soda, baking powder, sugar, and flour.
2. In a separate dish, whisk together the buttermilk, egg, melted butter, as well as vanilla essence.
3. Pour the wet ingredients into the dry components and stir until just combined.
4. Inside a small-sized bowl, mix together the melted butter, brown sugar, and ground cinnamon for the cinnamon swirl.
5. Preheat a griddle or skillet that doesn't require oil over a medium flame. Pour 1/4 cup of batter onto the skillet and spread it out into a circle.
6. Drizzle a tablespoon of the cinnamon swirl mixture onto the pancake batter. Use a toothpick or knife to swirl it into the batter.
7. Cook the pancake until bubbles form on the surface, then flip and cook until golden brown.
8. Repeat with the remaining batter and cinnamon swirl mixture.
9. In a mixing bowl, beat together the softened cream cheese, powdered sugar, and milk until smooth and creamy.
10. Serve the cinnamon roll pancakes warm with a drizzle of cream cheese glaze.

Nutrition Value (per serving): Calories: 380; Proteins: 10g; Carbs: 50g; Fats: 15g; Cholesterol: 70mg; Sodium: 500mg

13. CHERRY ALMOND BREAD

Prep Time: 20 minutes   **Total Time:** 3 hours 30 minutes   **Serving:** 1 loaf

INGREDIENTS

- 1 cup sourdough starter
- 1 1/2 cups bread flour
- 1 1/2 cups all-purpose flour
- 1/2 cup dried cherries
- 1/2 cup chopped almonds
- 1 teaspoon salt
- 1 tablespoon sugar
- 1 cup warm water
- 1/4 cup almond milk
- 2 tablespoons melted butter
- 1 teaspoon almond extract

DIRECTIONS

1. In a large mixing bowl, combine the sourdough starter, bread flour, all-purpose flour, dried cherries, chopped almonds, salt, and sugar.
2. Gradually add the warm water, almond milk, melted butter, and almond extract to the dry components. Mix until a sticky dough forms.
3. The dough should be kneaded on a floured surface for approximately five minutes, or until it is smooth and elastic.
4. Place the dough in a greased bowl, cover with a clean kitchen towel, and let it rise in a warm place for about 2-3 hours, or until size has more than doubled.
5. Preheat the oven to 375°F (190°C). Grease a loaf pan.
6. Punch down the dough and shape it into a loaf. Place the loaf into the prepared pan.
7. Cover the pan with the kitchen towel and let it rise for another 30 minutes.
8. The bread needs to be baked for 30-35 minutes in a preheated oven until it is golden and hollow once tapped on the bottom.
9. Remove the bread from the pan and let it cool completely on a wire rack before slicing.

Nutrition Value (per serving): Calories: 220; Proteins: 6g; Carbs: 35g; Fats: 6g; Cholesterol: 5mg; Sodium: 250mg

14. HERB AND CHEESE BISCUITS

Prep Time: 15 minutes   **Total Time:** 30 minutes   **Serving:** 12 biscuits

INGREDIENTS

- 2 cups flour
- 2 teaspoons baking powder
- 1/2 teaspoon baking soda
- 1/2 teaspoon salt
- 1/2 cup cold unsalted butter, cubed
- 1 cup sourdough starter
- 1/2 cup grated cheddar cheese
- 2 tablespoons chopped fresh herbs (such as parsley, chives, or thyme)
- 1/2 cup buttermilk

DIRECTIONS

1. Turn the oven temperature up to 425 degrees Fahrenheit (220 degrees Celsius). Prepare parchment paper on a baking pan.
2. In a huge dish, whisk together the baking soda, flour, baking powder, and salt.
3. Add the cold butter to the flour mixture and cut it in using a pastry cutter or your fingers to the point that the mixture resembles crushed crumbs.
4. Stir in the sourdough starter, grated cheddar cheese, and chopped fresh herbs until just combined.
5. Gradually add the buttermilk, stirring until the dough comes together. Be careful not to over mix.
6. To bring the dough together, turn it out onto a generously floured area and knead it a few times.
7. Pat the dough into a 1-inch thick rectangle and cut out biscuits using a biscuit cutter or a glass.
8. Place the biscuits on the prepared baking sheet, leaving a small gap between each biscuit.
9. Bake for 12-15 minutes, or until the biscuits are golden brown.
10. Remove out of your oven let the biscuits cool slightly before serving.

Nutrition Value (per serving): Calories: 180; Proteins: 5g; Carbs: 20g; Fats: 9g; Cholesterol: 25mg; Sodium: 350mg

15. RASPBERRY MUFFINS

Prep Time: 15 minutes   **Total Time:** 35 minutes   **Serving:** 12 muffins

INGREDIENTS

- 2 cups of flour
- 1/2 cup sugar
- 1/2 teaspoon of baking soda
- 1 cup sourdough starter
- 1/2 cup milk
- 1 egg
- 1/4 cup melted butter
- 1 teaspoon vanilla extract
- 1/2 teaspoon of salt
- 1 cup fresh or frozen raspberries
- 2 teaspoons of baking powder

DIRECTIONS

1. Preheat the oven to 375°F (190°C). Grease a muffin tin or line with paper liners.
2. In a huge dish, whisk together salt, baking soda, baking powder, sugar, and flour.
3. In a separate bowl, mix together the sourdough starter, milk, melted butter, vanilla extract, and egg.
4. Combine the dry and wet components by pouring the wet into the dry and stirring together. Do not over-blend.
5. Gently fold in the raspberries.
6. Divide the batter evenly among the muffin cups, filling each about 2/3 full.
7. Bake for 18-20 minutes, or when a toothpick is put into the center of a muffin arrives clear.
8. Remove the muffins from the tin and let them cool on a wire rack.

Nutrition Value (per serving): Calories: 180; Proteins: 4g; Carbs: 30g; Fats: 5g; Cholesterol: 30mg; Sodium: 300mg

16. BUTTERMILK PANCAKES

Prep Time: 10 minutes   **Total Time:** 25 minutes   **Serving:** 4

INGREDIENTS

- 1 cup sourdough starter
- 1/2 teaspoon of baking soda
- 1 cup flour
- 1 tablespoon sugar
- 1 teaspoon of baking powder
- 1/2 teaspoon salt
- 1 cup buttermilk
- 1 egg
- 2 tablespoons melted butter

DIRECTIONS

1. In a huge bowl, combine the sourdough starter, salt, baking soda, baking powder, sugar, and flour.
2. In a separate dish, whisk together the buttermilk, egg, and melted butter.
3. Combine the dry and wet components by pouring the wet into the dry and stirring together.
4. Warm a non-stick skillet or griddle on medium flame.
5. Pour 1/4 cup of batter onto the skillet for each pancake and spread it out into a circle.
6. Cook the pancake until bubbles form on the surface, then flip and cook until golden brown.
7. Repeat with the remaining batter.
8. Serve the pancakes warm with your favorite toppings such as maple syrup, berries, or whipped cream.

Nutrition Value (per serving): Calories: 220; Proteins: 8g; Carbs: 30g; Fats: 7g; Cholesterol: 60mg; Sodium: 550mg

17. SUN-DRIED TOMATO AND BASIL BREAD

Prep Time: 25 minutes   **Total Time:** 4 hours 15 minutes   **Serving:** 1 loaf

INGREDIENTS

- 1 cup sourdough starter
- 2 1/2 cups bread flour
- 1/2 cup whole wheat flour
- 1 1/2 teaspoons salt
- 1/4 cup chopped sun-dried tomatoes (packed in oil)
- 2 tablespoons chopped fresh basil
- 1 1/4 cups warm water

DIRECTIONS

1. In a large mixing bowl, combine the sourdough starter, bread flour, whole wheat flour, salt, chopped sun-dried tomatoes, and chopped fresh basil.
2. Gradually add the warm water to the mixture, stirring until a shaggy dough forms.
3. Turn the dough out onto a board that has been lightly dusted with flour and knead for about 10 minutes, until elastic and smooth.
4. Place the dough in a greased bowl, cover with a clean kitchen towel, and let it rise in a warm place for about 3-4 hours, or until size has more than doubled.
5. Preheat the oven to 450°F (230°C). Place a Dutch oven or oven-safe pot with a lid in the oven while it preheats.
6. Carefully remove the hot pot out of your oven transfer the risen dough into it. Score the top of the dough with a sharp knife.
7. Cover the pot with the lid and bake for 30 minutes.
8. Remove the lid and continue baking for an additional 15-20 minutes, or until the bread is golden brown.
9. Remove the bread from the pot and let it cool completely on a wire rack before slicing.

Nutrition Value (per serving): Calories: 210; Proteins: 8g; Carbs: 42g; Fats: 1g; Cholesterol: 0mg; Sodium: 350mg

18. DOUBLE CHOCOLATE PANCAKES

Prep Time: 15 minutes   **Total Time:** 25 minutes   **Serving:** 4

INGREDIENTS

- 1/2 cup of chocolate chips
- 1 cup sourdough starter
- 1/2 teaspoon of baking soda
- 1 cup flour
- 2 tablespoons of melted butter
- 1/4 cup unsweetened cocoa powder
- 1 cup of buttermilk
- 1/4 cup sugar
- 1 teaspoon of baking powder
- 1/2 teaspoon of salt
- 1 egg

DIRECTIONS

1. Inside a large-sized bowl, combine the sourdough starter, flour, cocoa powder, sugar, baking powder, salt and baking soda.
2. In a separate dish, whisk the egg, buttermilk, and melted butter.
3. Combine the dry and wet components by pouring the wet into the dry and stirring together.
4. Incorporate the melted chocolate.
5. Heat a non-stick skillet or griddle over medium flame.
6. Pour 1/4 cup of batter onto the skillet for each pancake and spread it out into a circle.
7. Cook the pancake until bubbles create on the surface, then flip and cook until cooked through.
8. Repeat with the remainder of batter.
9. Serve the pancakes warm with additional chocolate chips and your favorite toppings, such as whipped cream or berries.

Nutrition Value (per serving): Calories: 320; Proteins: 9g; Carbs: 48g; Fats: 12g; Cholesterol: 70mg; Sodium: 550mg

19. PECAN CRANBERRY BREAD

Prep Time: 25 minutes   **Total Time:** 4 hours 30 minutes   **Serving:** 1 loaf

INGREDIENTS

- 1 cup sourdough starter
- 2 1/2 cups bread flour
- 1/2 cup whole wheat flour
- 1 1/2 teaspoons salt
- 1/2 cup dried cranberries
- 1/2 cup chopped pecans
- 1 1/4 cups warm water

DIRECTIONS

1. In a large mixing bowl, combine the sourdough starter, bread flour, whole wheat flour, salt, dried cranberries, and chopped pecans.
2. Gradually add the warm water to the mixture, stirring until a shaggy dough forms.
3. Turn the dough out onto a board that has been lightly dusted with flour and knead for about 10 minutes, until elastic and smooth.
4. Place the dough in a greased bowl, cover with a clean kitchen towel, and let it rise in a warm place for about 3-4 hours, or until size has more than doubled.
5. Preheat the oven to 450°F (230°C). Place a Dutch oven or oven-safe pot with a lid in the oven while it preheats.
6. Carefully remove the hot pot out of your oven transfer the risen dough into it. Score the top of the dough with a sharp knife.
7. Cover the pot with the lid and bake for 30 minutes.
8. Remove the lid and continue baking for an additional 15-20 minutes, or until the bread is golden brown.
9. Remove the bread from the pot and let it cool completely on a wire rack before slicing.

Nutrition Value (per serving): Calories: 220; Proteins: 7g; Carbs: 42g; Fats: 3g; Cholesterol: 0mg; Sodium: 350mg

20. SPINACH AND FETA MUFFINS

Prep Time: 15 minutes   **Total Time:** 35 minutes   **Serving:** 12 muffins

INGREDIENTS

- 2 cups flour
- 2 teaspoons baking powder
- 1/2 teaspoon of baking soda
- 1 cup sourdough starter
- 1/2 cup milk
- 1/4 cup melted butter
- 2 eggs
- 1/2 teaspoon of salt
- 1 cup chopped spinach
- 1/2 cup crumbled feta cheese

DIRECTIONS

1. Preheat the oven to 375°F (190°C). Grease a muffin tin or line with paper liners.
2. In a huge dish, whisk together the baking soda, flour, baking powder, and salt.
3. In a separate bowl, mix together the sourdough starter, milk, melted butter, and eggs.
4. Pour the wet ingredients into the dry components and stir until just combined. Do not over mix.
5. Gently fold in the chopped spinach and crumbled feta cheese.
6. Divide the batter evenly among the muffin cups, filling each about 2/3 full.
7. Bake for 18-20 minutes, or when a toothpick is put into the center of a muffin arrives clear.
8. Remove the muffins from the tin and let them cool on a wire rack.

Nutrition Value (per serving): Calories: 160; Proteins: 5g; Carbs: 22g; Fats: 6g; Cholesterol: 45mg; Sodium: 350mg

21. CARAMELIZED ONION AND GRUYERE BREAD

Prep Time: 25 minutes   **Total Time:** 4 hours 30 minutes   **Serving:** 1 loaf

INGREDIENTS

- 1 cup sourdough starter
- 2 1/2 cups bread flour
- 1/2 cup whole wheat flour
- 1 1/2 teaspoons salt
- 2 onions, thinly sliced
- 2 tablespoons butter
- 1 cup shredded Gruyere cheese
- 1 1/4 cups warm water

DIRECTIONS

1. In a large mixing bowl, combine the sourdough starter, bread flour, whole wheat flour, and salt.
2. Gradually add the warm water to the mixture, stirring until a shaggy dough forms.
3. Turn the dough out onto a board that has been lightly dusted with flour and knead for about 10 minutes, until elastic and smooth.
4. Place the dough in a greased bowl, cover with a clean kitchen towel, and let it rise in a warm place for about 3-4 hours, or until size has more than doubled.
5. While the dough is rising, heat the butter in a skillet with moderate heat. Add the thinly sliced onions and cook until caramelized, stirring occasionally. Set aside to cool.
6. Preheat the oven to 450°F (230°C). Place a Dutch oven or oven-safe pot with a lid in the oven while it preheats.
7. Carefully remove the hot pot out of your oven transfer the risen dough into it. Score the top of the dough with a sharp knife.
8. Spread the caramelized onions and shredded Gruyere cheese evenly over the dough.
9. Cover the pot with the lid and bake for 30 minutes.
10. Remove the lid and continue baking for an additional 15-20 minutes, or until the bread is golden brown and the cheese is melted and bubbly.
11. Remove the bread from the pot and let it cool completely on a wire rack before slicing.

Nutrition Value (per serving): Calories: 240; Proteins: 9g; Carbs: 43g; Fats: 5g; Cholesterol: 20mg; Sodium: 400mg

22. BUTTER BLUEBERRY PANCAKES

Prep Time: 10 minutes   **Total Time:** 25 minutes   **Serving:** 4

INGREDIENTS

- 1 cup of fresh blueberries
- 1/4 teaspoon of salt
- 1 tablespoon of sugar
- 1/2 teaspoon baking powder
- 1 cup of flour
- 1/2 teaspoon of baking soda
- 1 cup of sourdough starter
- 2 tablespoons of melted butter
- 1 large egg
- 1/2 cup of milk

DIRECTIONS

1. In a huge dish, whisk together the salt, baking soda, baking powder, sugar, and flour.
2. In a separate bowl, combine the sourdough starter, milk, egg, and melted butter. Whisk until well combined.
3. Pour the wet ingredients into the dry components and stir until just combined. Gently fold in the blueberries.
4. Prepare a pan or griddle by heating it on the stovetop while lightly oiled. For each pancake, use about a quarter cup of batter.
5. Cook until small bubbles form on the surface of the pancakes, then flip and cook for an additional 1-2 minutes, until golden brown.
6. Serve the pancakes warm with maple syrup or your desired toppings.

Nutrition Value (per serving): Calories: 250; Proteins: 7g; Carbs: 39g; Fats: 7g; Cholesterol: 55mg; Sodium: 400mg

23. QUICK NAAN BREAD

Prep Time: 10 minutes   **Total Time:** 1 hour 30 minutes   **Serving:** 6

INGREDIENTS

- 1 cup of sourdough starter
- 1/4 teaspoon of baking powder
- 2 cups flour
- 1/2 teaspoon of salt
- 1 tablespoon of olive oil
- 1/2 cup of plain yogurt
- 2 tablespoons of melted butter (for brushing)

DIRECTIONS

1. In a large bowl, combine the sourdough starter, flour, salt, baking powder, yogurt, and olive oil. Mix until the dough comes together.
2. For about five minutes on a surface dusted with flour, knead the dough until it is smooth and elastic.
3. Place the dough in a greased bowl, cover with a damp cloth, and let it rise for 1 hour.
4. After the dough has risen, divide it into 6 equal portions. Roll out each portion into a thin circle.
5. Heat a skillet or griddle over medium-high heat. Cook each naan bread for about 2 minutes on each side, until puffed and golden.
6. Brush the cooked naan bread with melted butter and serve warm.

Nutrition Value (per serving): Calories: 220; Proteins: 6g; Carbs: 35g; Fats: 6g; Cholesterol: 15mg; Sodium: 320mg

24. BANANA NUT BREAD

Prep Time: 15 minutes   **Total Time:** 1 hour 30 minutes   **Serving:** 10

INGREDIENTS

- 1/2 teaspoon ground cinnamon
- 1/4 teaspoon of ground nutmeg
- 1/2 cup of brown sugar
- 1 3/4 cups of all-purpose flour
- 1 teaspoon of baking soda
- 1 cup ripe bananas, mashed
- 1/2 cup sourdough starter
- 1/3 cup vegetable oil
- 2 large eggs
- 1/2 cup of granulated sugar
- 1/2 teaspoon of salt
- 1 teaspoon vanilla extract
- 1/2 cup chopped walnuts

DIRECTIONS

1. Turn the oven temperature up to 350 degrees Fahrenheit (175 degrees Celsius). Coat a 9-by-5-inch loaf pan with butter and flour.
2. Mix the cinnamon, flour, salt, baking soda, and nutmeg in a medium bowl.
3. Mix the mashed bananas, eggs, sourdough starter, brown sugar, granulated sugar, oil, and vanilla extract in a separate large basin. Combine all of the components thoroughly.
4. Add dry ingredients to wet and stir until combined.
5. Incorporate the chopped walnuts.
6. Then, pour the mixture into the pan and level the top.
7. Bake for 50 to 60 minutes, or till a toothpick put in the middle comes out clear.
8. After ten minutes, remove the bread from the pan and place it on a wire rack for cooling entirely.

Nutrition Value (per serving): Calories: 280; Proteins: 5g; Carbs: 41g; Fats: 11g; Cholesterol: 35mg; Sodium: 320mg

25. HERB FLATBREAD

Prep Time: 15 minutes   **Total Time:** 40 minutes   **Serving:** 8

INGREDIENTS

- 1/4 teaspoon of dried thyme
- 1 cup sourdough starter
- 1 1/2 cups all-purpose flour
- 1/4 teaspoon garlic powder
- 1/4 teaspoon dried basil
- 1/2 teaspoon of salt
- 1/4 teaspoon dried oregano
- 2 tablespoons olive oil

DIRECTIONS

1. In a large bowl, combine the sourdough starter, flour, salt, garlic powder, basil, oregano, and thyme. Mix until a dough forms.
2. Flour a work surface and knead the dough for a few minutes till it is smooth.
3. Divide the dough into 4 equal portions and roll each portion into a thin circle.
4. Heat a skillet or griddle over medium-high heat. Brush each flatbread with olive oil and cook for about 2-3 minutes on each side, until golden brown.
5. Remove from the heat and let them cool slightly before serving.

Nutrition Value (per serving): Calories: 160; Proteins: 4g; Carbs: 27g; Fats: 4g; Cholesterol: 0mg; Sodium: 160mg

MEASUREMENT CONVERSION CHART

CUP	OUNCES	MILLILITERS	TABLESPOONS
8 cup	64 oz.	1895 ml	128
6 cup	48 oz.	1420 ml	96
5 cup	40 oz.	1180 ml	80
4 cup	32 oz.	960 ml	64
2 cup	16 oz.	480 ml	32
1 cup	8 oz.	240 ml	16
3/4 cup	6 oz.	177 ml	12
2/3 cup	5 oz.	158 ml	11
1/2 cup	4 oz.	118 ml	8
3/8 cup	3 oz.	90 ml	6
1/3 cup	2.5 oz.	79 ml	5.5
1/4 cup	2 oz.	59 ml	4
1/8 cup	1 oz.	30 ml	3
1/16 cup	1/2 oz.	15 ml	1

CONCLUSION

In the realm of sourdough baking, we have embarked on an extraordinary odyssey filled with mouthwatering delights and tantalizing aromas. From fluffy pancakes that dance on your taste buds to rustic loaves that transport you to a rustic countryside, this cookbook has been a gateway to a culinary wonderland.

But this adventure goes beyond the realm of mere recipes. It is a journey of discovery, where science and history converge to unlock the secrets of sourdough's captivating allure. We have unraveled the mysteries of wild yeast, harnessed the power of fermentation, and tapped into the ancient wisdom passed down through generations of bakers. It is a testament to the transformative nature of time, patience, and the alchemy of flavors.

Sourdough baking isn't just about satisfying our cravings; it's about nourishing our bodies and souls. It's about embracing the rich tapestry of flavors, textures, and health benefits that sourdough offers. The slow fermentation process not only creates bread that is deeply satisfying to the senses but also enhances digestibility and unleashes a myriad of nutrients that are easily absorbed by our bodies. It's a harmonious dance between our taste buds and our well-being.

As we've journeyed through this cookbook, we've encountered challenges and overcome them with grace. We've learned to troubleshoot, adapt, and create our own unique twists on classic recipes. The path to sourdough mastery is paved with resilience, experimentation, and a dash of audacity. It's about embracing the unexpected and celebrating the imperfect beauty that emerges from our ovens.

Now armed with the knowledge, techniques, and recipes from this cookbook, you are ready to forge your own path in the world of sourdough. Let your imagination run wild as you infuse your creations with your personal touch. Explore different grains, add spices and fruits, and push the boundaries of flavor. The possibilities are as endless as your creativity.

But let's not forget the true essence of sourdough baking: sharing the fruits of our labor with loved ones. There is magic in breaking bread together, in the laughter and stories that unfold around a table filled with warm, fragrant loaves. It's a celebration of community, love, and the sheer joy of creating something delicious from scratch.

As we conclude this journey, remember that sourdough baking is a lifelong pursuit. It's a symphony of flavors that evolves and deepens over time. Embrace the process, relish the lessons, and savor the fruits of your labor. The aroma of freshly baked sourdough will forever be a beacon, calling you back to the heart of your kitchen.

So, with aprons tied and oven mitts at the ready, go forth and let your sourdough creations dazzle and inspire. May your loaves be crusty, your pancakes be fluffy, and your desserts be a sweet symphony of flavors. This is your time to shine as a sourdough artist, to make your mark on the world, one delectable bite at a time.

Happy baking!

GLOSSARY

Autolyse: A resting period after mixing flour and water, allowing gluten development and enzyme activity.

Bulk Fermentation: The initial fermentation period where the dough rises, develops flavor, and increases in volume.

Bench Rest: A short rest period after bulk fermentation, allowing the dough to relax and become easier to shape.

Crumb: The interior texture and structure of the bread, ranging from open and airy to tight and dense.

Crust: The outer layer of the bread that forms during baking, varying in color and texture.

Enzymes: Natural substances present in flour that break down complex carbohydrates and proteins during fermentation, influencing flavor and texture.

Fermentation: A metabolic process in which microorganisms, such as yeast or bacteria, convert sugars into alcohol, acids, or gases in the absence of oxygen. It is a natural process that has been used for centuries to produce various foods and beverages.

Fold: A technique used during bulk fermentation to strengthen the dough's structure and improve its texture.

Gluten Development: The process of forming a network of gluten proteins in the dough, which provides structure and elasticity.

Lactobacilli: A type of bacteria that produces lactic acid during fermentation, contributing to the tangy flavor in sourdough.

Lame: A tool with a razor blade used for scoring the dough in a sourdough recipe.

Levain: A portion of the starter that is built up and used to leaven the dough in a sourdough recipe.

Proofing: The final fermentation stage where the shaped dough undergoes its final rise before baking.

Rustic: A style of bread that embodies a more traditional, country-style aesthetic and flavor.

Sourdough: A naturally fermented bread made from a combination of flour and water, with the aid of wild yeast and lactobacilli bacteria.

Starter: A mixture of flour and water that captures and cultivates wild yeast and bacteria, used as a leavening agent in sourdough baking.

Scoring: Making cuts or slashes on the surface of the dough just before baking, allowing it to expand and create a beautiful pattern.

Shaping: The process of forming the dough into its desired shape, such as boules, batards, or baguettes.

Sourdough Discard: The portion of the starter that is removed and discarded during feeding, often used in recipes to add flavor and tang.

Wild Yeast: Natural yeast present in the environment that is captured and cultivated to leaven sourdough bread.

Thank you from the bottom of my heart for choosing to read this book!

It is with immense gratitude that I address these words to you. It gives me enormous pleasure to know that you have decided to give your time and attention to these pages that I have written with commitment and dedication.

Creating this book has been an exciting journey, and my hope is that you have found it as enjoyable and inspiring to read as I have in writing it. Every word was carefully chosen with the goal of conveying a message, a story or a new perspective to you.

I am aware that you have a multitude of choices available to you when it comes to books, and the fact that you chose mine is a source of great pride and happiness. Your choice is invaluable to me, as it is the support and interest of readers like you that give meaning to my work as a writer.

If you have enjoyed the journey you have taken with these pages, I kindly ask you to **share your experience with others**. Reader reviews are a vital tool for raising awareness of a book and helping other readers make an informed choice.

If you feel inspired to do so, you might **take a few minutes to write a positive review** in which you could share your opinions. Even a few words can make a huge difference and help introduce the book to a wider audience.

INDEX OF RECIPES